중학 내신만점

영문법 쏙쏙·영어 쑥쑥

바다편

저자 동영상 강의 예정
www.seeenglish.com

시잉글리쉬
www.seeenglish.com

중학 내신만점
영문법 쏙쏙 · 영어 쑥쑥 (바다편)

초판 발행: 2016년 1.1일

지은이 · 손 창 연
펴낸이 · 손 창 연
표지디자인 · 전 철 규
내지디자인 · 필커뮤니케이션
인쇄 · 송죽문화사
펴낸곳 · **시잉글리쉬**
서울 서초구 양재동 106-6 정오 B/D 402호(우 137-891)
Tel: [02] 573-3581
등록번호 제 22- 2733호
Homepage: **www.seeenglish.com**

ISBN:

정가: 13,000원

들어가는 _ 말

무엇이든 기본이 중요하다.

영어를 가르치기 시작한지도 20여년이 넘었다. 그 동안 중고생들과 대학생 및 성인 등에게 TOEFL, TOEIC, 편입영어, 수능, 중고생 내신 등을 가르치면서 느낀 점은 역시 '기본이 중요하다'라는 것이다. 특히 영어문법은 처음 시작할 때 제대로 배워야 한다는 생각이다.

이 책은 영어를 학습하는 중학생을 위한 책이다. 상위권 초등 5,6학년에게도 어렵지 않다. 학교 영어수업을 이해하고 영어시험에 빈틈없이 준비할 수 있도록 했다. 또한 영어의 기본을 확실하게 하고자 했다.

모든 공부나 세상의 일들이 그렇듯이 영어라는 바다에 나가 자유롭게 항해하기 위해서는 영어단어 하나하나를 꼼꼼히 읽히고, 아주 기초적인 문장에 대한 이치를 정확하게 읽혔을 때, 풍랑에도 안전하게 항해 할 수 있는 진정한 영어실력을 갖출 수 있다.

로마가 하루 아침에 이루어 지지 않았듯이(Rome wasn't built in a day.) 영어도 하루 아침에 이루어 질 수 있는 것이 아니다. 긴 시간동안 끊임없는 암기와 이해, 반복적인 학습이 필요하다.

이 책에서 제시하는 내용을 꼼꼼히 잘 읽히고 문제를 풀어나가다 보면, 자기도 모르는 사이 영어실력이 부쩍 늘었다는 것을 알게 될 것이다.

끝으로 이 책으로 학습하는 모든 학생들이 단 한번 밖에 없는 인생에서 자신의 꿈을 이루고, 인류의 평화와 자유, 그리고 민주주의를 위해 각각의 그릇에 맞는 기여를 하길 기원한다.

2016년 1월 1일

저자 손 창 언

쫄지 말고 열공 ^^

[이 책을 이렇게 공부하자.]

◆ 학습자의 수준에 따라 다르겠지만 작은 챕터는 하루에 하나 긴 챕터는 2~3일에 정복해보자.

◆ 각 챕터의 핵심개념을 정확히 이해 한다. 또 해당 예문을 꼼꼼히 익힌다.

◆ '**확인문제**'를 통하여 핵심개념을 심화하고 순발력을 강화한다. '**확인문제**' 문장들도 문제의 답을 찾는데 그치지 않고 각각 해석도 해본다. 언어는 의미파악이 주요 목적이고 문법은 그 의미를 정확하게 하기 위함이다.

◆ '**Reading in Grammar**'에서 문제를 풀면서 독해속에서 활용을 해본다.

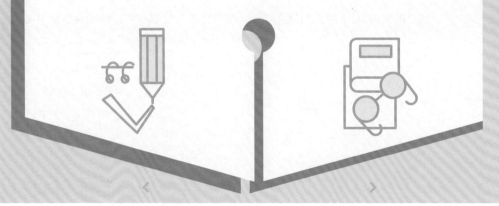

◆ **'중간·기말고사 내신만점대비문제'**를 풀면서 다시 한번 보다 치밀하게 학습한다.

◆ **별책 단어책**의 단원별 단어들을 꼼꼼히 학습하자. 영어학습에서 빼놓을 수 없는 것이 어휘이다. 아무리 설계가 좋고 높은 건물일지라도 벽돌 등 하나하나의 자재 없이 건물은 완성 될 수 없기 때문이다.

◆ 마지막으로 최고의 학습법이자 성공의 팁은 **끈기**다.

기억하자!

[느리지만 꾸준히만 한다면 이길 수 있다.]

Slow but steady wins the race.

Structure

이 책의 _ **구성**

문법핵심 정리와 해설

문법을 이해하기 위한 핵심적인
내용을 예문과 함께 설명했다.

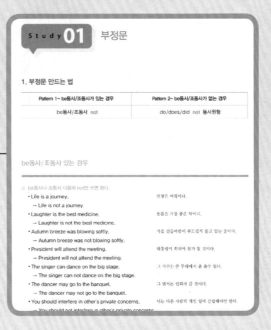

확인문제

문법핵심내용을 확인하고 활용하도록
핵심내용을 문제로 풀어보도록 했다.

Grammar in Reading

배운 내용을 쉬운 지문의 독해속에서
도 활용할 수 있도록 어법상 맞지 않는
것을 찾는 문장 등의 문법문제를 출제
했다.

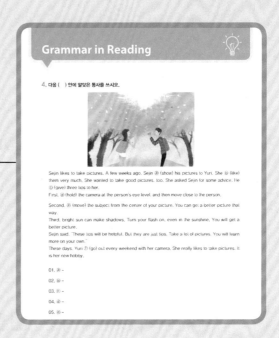

중간 · 기말고사
내신만점대비문제

각 단원에서 배운 문법내용을 다시
한번 점검하고 영작 등으로 응용할 수
있도록 했다.
이를 통해 학교 내신시험에 철저히
대비할 수 있는 힘을 기르도록 했다.

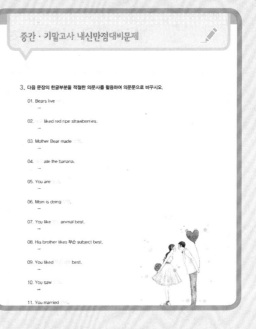

이 책의 _ **차례**

Contents

중학내신만점 영문법 쏙쏙 · 영어 쑥쑥   **바다편**

부록

Solution (정답과 해설)

Contents

이 책의 _ **차례**

별 책

중학내신만점
영문법 쏙쏙 · 영어 쑥쑥 [땅편]

땅 편

중학내신만점
영문법 쏙쏙 · 영어 쑥쑥 [하늘편]

하늘편

Chapter

01

Making Verbs
for present

현재형동사 만들기

‖ 주어가 3인칭 단수일 때, 현재형동사 만들기

주어가 3인칭 단수일 때, 현재형동사 만드는 방법

주어가 3인칭 단수일 때, 일반적으로 동사원형에 –(e)s 붙인다.

<table>
<tr>
<td colspan="3">동사원형 + s: 아래 특별한 경우를 제외하고 대부분의 경우</td>
<td>play → plays
make → makes
lie → lies
bake → bakes</td>
</tr>
<tr>
<td rowspan="4">-s를 붙이지 않는
특별한 경우</td>
<td rowspan="3">-es
붙이는경우</td>
<td>발음이
[s][z][ʃ][ʧ][ʤ]
(수저쉬취쥐로암기)</td>
<td>다만 이경우도 –e로
끝나는 경우는 그냥
–s만 붙인다.</td>
<td>miss → misses
pass → passes
guess → guesses
discuss → discusses
buzz → buzzes
reach → reaches
cf> –e로 끝나는 경우
close → closes
dance → dances
change → changes</td>
</tr>
<tr>
<td>자음+y로 끝날 때</td>
<td>y를 i로 고치고 –es
cf> 다만 모음+y일
때는 그냥 –s만 쓴다.</td>
<td>cry → cries
fly → flies
worry → worries
hurry → hurries
cf> 모음 + y
pay → pays
buy → buys</td>
</tr>
<tr>
<td>자음+o</td>
<td></td>
<td>go → goes
do → does</td>
</tr>
<tr>
<td colspan="2">* 특별한 3인칭 단수형</td>
<td>be동사</td>
<td>is</td>
</tr>
</table>

		have동사	has

1. –es를 붙이는 경우

① 발음이 [s], [z], [ʃ], [ʧ], [ʤ](수저쉬취쥐로 암기)로 끝나는 단어

teach → teaches 가르치다	brush → brushes 솔질하다	guess → guesses 추측하다
buzz → buzzes 윙윙거리다	reach → reaches 도달하다	pass → passes 지나가다
quiz → quizes 퀴즈 내다	fix → fixes 고치다	

cf> 다만 위의 [s], [z], [ʃ], [ʧ], [ʤ]('수저시치지'로 암기)발음으로 끝나지만 단어의 끝이 –e인 경우는 –s만 붙인다.

close → closes 닫다	dance → dances 춤추다	change → changes 변화하다

② 철자가 '자음+y'로 끝날 때 y를 i로 고치고 –es를 붙인다.

fly → flies 날다	try → tries 노력하다	worry → worries 걱정하다
marry → marries 결혼하다	apply → applies 적용하다	copy → copies 복사하다

cf> 하지만 '모음+y'로 끝나는 경우는 s만을 붙인다.

play → plays 놀다	pay → pays 지불하다	buy → buys 사다

③ 철자가 '자음+o'로 끝날 때

go → goes do → does

2. 위의 ①,②,③의 –es를 붙이는 것을 제외하면 나머지는 모두 –s를 붙인다.

meet → meets 만나다	fight → fights 싸우다	want → wants 원하다

3. 특별한 3인칭 단수형

be 동사	is	have동사	has

 확인문제 1

주어가 3인칭 단수일 때 다음 단어들의 현재형을 쓰시오.

(01). have →   (02). be →

(03). put →   (04). stop →

(05). work →   (06). beg →

(07). pass →   (08). quiz →

(09). fix →   (10). go →

(11). play →   (12). marry →

(13). apply →   (14). pay →

(15). copy →   (16). try →

(17). cry →   (18). fly →

(19). wash →   (20). finish →

〈정답과 해설 2P〉

 확인문제 2

주어가 3인칭 단수일 때 다음 단어들의 현재형을 쓰시오.

(01). reach →   (02). study →

(03). mix →   (04). run →

(05). work →   (06). walk →

(07). jump →   (08). sit →

(09). hop →   (10). meet →

(11). depart →   (12). face →

(13). reduce →   (14). relax →

(15). teach →   (16). sing →

(17). reward →   (18). miss →

(19). decrease →   (20). destroy →

〈정답과 해설 2P〉

Grammar in Reading

〈정답과 해설 2P〉

1. 다음 글을 읽고 어법상 맞지 않는 것을 모두 찾아 올바로 고치시오.

Alex like going to a fast food restaurant to eat hamburgers and French fries. His mother always tell him to stop eating junk food. He also think that eating junk food are unhealthy. He know it's hard to stop it, but he'll tries.

2. 다음 글을 읽고 어법상 맞지 않는 것을 모두 찾아 올바로 고치시오.

The Earth are full of plastic bags. They can causes serious problems. For example, many turtles is killed by plastic bags. They eats the bags because they thinks the bags is fish. What can we does? Perhaps the easiest way to begin are recycling them. Here is some tips.

3. 다음 글을 읽고 어법상 맞지 않는 것을 모두 찾아 올바로 고치시오

Can you imagines your life without energy? Our lives would is different without it. Energy are very important in our lives. It do many things for us. Energy give us the power to turn on our light. It keep our food fresh. It also keep us warm and cool.

Grammar in Reading

〈정답과 해설 3P〉

4. 다음 글을 읽고 어법상 맞지 않는 것을 모두 찾아 올바로 고치시오.

[Allie goes out.]

Marie Curie: You doesn't understand me.
All my wishes is gone! I'm not happy!
Genie: Wishes are not the key to your happiness.

[Genie goes out and Marie Curie fall into a chair. Jesi comes back. She comes up to Marie Curie and talk to him.]
Jesi: I'm looking for my keys. Can you help me?

Marie Curie: Keys?
Jesi: Oh, here they are.
Marie Curie: Well, let me to introduce myself.
Jesi: I know your name, Marie Curie. My name is Jesi.
Marie Curie: I'm glad to meet you, Jesi. Well, why don't we go for a bike ride? It's a beautiful day.
Jesi: Sure, I like bike riding.

[Jesi and Marie Curie goes out. Genie comes in and smile.]
Genie: Now Marie Curie found a right girl for him. And how about you, Jesi? Are you happy with this?

Grammar in Reading

〈정답과 해설 3~4P〉

5. 다음 글을 읽고 어법상 맞지 않는 것을 모두 찾아 올바로 고치시오.

[In a computer room, Jesi is using a computer. Derek comes in.]

Jesi: Hi. How are you do?

[Derek don't hear her. He go to a computer and start working.
Jesi gets upset and walk out. Derek finds a CD in the computer. It comes out slowly. He looks at it and clean it with cloth. Genie comes in.]

Genie: What do you wants?
Derek: What? Who are you?
Genie: I'm Genie.
Derek: Genie? So ... I can get three wish?
Genie: Yeah, yeah. You know the Aladdin story, right?
Derek: Cool. Oh, I want a perfect girlfriend.
Genie: As you wish ..

〈정답과 해설 4P〉

1. 주어가 3인칭 단수일 때 다음 단어들의 현재형을 쓰시오.

01. tell →   02. produce →

03. breathe →   04. make →

05. change →   06. shoot →

07. like →   08. bite →

09. answer →   10. ask →

11. use →   12. open →

13. close →   14. depend →

15. rely →   16. lie →

17. wait →   18. sing →

19. dance →   20. fight →

2. 다음 문장의 (   ) 안에 동사의 현재형을 쓰시오.

01. My eyes (water).

02. The phone (ring).

03. The panic (spread).

04. Soccer (spread) hope

05. The situation (worsen).

〈정답과 해설 4P〉

06. The protest (turn) violent.

07. Nicolette and his friends (love) soccer.

08. Mom (stay) awake all night.

09. My son (wash) the dishes.

10. The professor (teach) Germany.

11. A girl (worry) about her grade.

12. The honor student (study) math hard.

13. A butterfly (fly) over the flowers.

14. Hellen (want) to have a better friend.

15. English (help) me make friends.

16. The king (want) to conquer land.

17. You (have) no right to stay here.

18. Habits (be) like second nature.

19. Dad (brush) his teeth three times a day.

20. The volunteers (want) to help more.

3. 다음 문장의 ( ) 안에 동사의 현재형을 쓰시오.

01. The workers (fall) from a high place.

〈정답과 해설 4P〉

02. Computer addicts often (skip) meals.

03. The snakes (survive) in the winter.

04. The vegetable (survive) the heavy snow.

05. Overwork (lead) to health problems.

06. A person (become) uneasy or upset.

07. A long journey (start) with the first step.

08. The student (want) to get better grades.

09. Korean's morning (begin) in Dokdo.

10. This engineer (fix) a car easily.

11. The customer (pay) his bill in cash.

12. The teacher (quiz) 10 questions every class.

13. The bus (pass) the bus stop at ten o'clock.

14. He usually (enjoy) the same kinds of foods that his family likes.

15. The reporter (carry) a camera and a notebook computer.

Chapter

02

Making plural of Nouns
복수형명사 만들기

‖ 2개 이상의 복수형명사 만들기

2개 이상의 명사, 복수형 만들기

동사원형에 –(e)s를 붙이는 3인칭 단수 현재형을 만드는 원리와 같다. 셀 수 있는 명사는 2개 이상을 나타내는 복수형을 만들 수 있다. 일반적으로 –s나 –(e)s를 붙인다.

명사 +s	아래 –es를 붙이는 경우를 제외하고 대부분의 경우	boy → boys 소년 girl → girls 소녀 computer →computers 컴퓨터 phone → phones 전화 animal → animals 동물
–es붙이는 특별한 경우	발음이 [s][z][ʃ][ʧ][ʤ] 로 끝날때 ※ (수저쉬취쥐로 암기)	fox → foxes 여우 bus → buses 버스 dish → dishes 접시
	자음+y로 끝날 때: y를 i로 고치고 es cf>모음+y는 그냥 s만	fly → flies 파리 city → cities 도시 cf> 모음 + y toy → toys 장난감 monkey → monkeys 원숭이
	자음+o 로 끝날 때 다만 모음+o는 그냥 –s	tomato → tomatoes 토마토 potato → potatoes 감자 cf> 모음 + o zoo → zoos 동물원
	–f(e)로 끝날 때 –f(e)를 -v로 고치고 –es	leaf → leaves 잎 knife → knives 칼

1. –es를 붙이는 경우

① 발음이 [s], [z], [ʃ], [tʃ], [ʤ]('수저시치지'로 암기)로 끝날때

glass-glasses 잔	fox-foxes 여우	punch-punches 주먹	address-addresses 주소
bus-buses 버스	church-churches 교회	bench-benches 벤치	match-matches 경기
wish-wishes 소망	box-boxes 상자	brush-brushes 솔	watch-watches 시계
toothbrush-toothbrushes 칫솔		sandwich-sandwiches 샌드위치	

다만 위의 [s], [z], [ʃ], [tʃ], [ʤ]('수저시치지'로 암기)발음으로 끝나지만 단어의 끝이 –e인 경우는 –s만 붙인다.

maze-mazes 미로	house-houses 집	piece-pieces 조각	blouse-blouses 블라우스

② 철자가 '자음 +y'로 끝날 때 y를 i로 고치고

fly-flies 파리	copy-copies 복사본	family-families 가족	baby-babies 아기
city-cities 도시	country-countries 국가	candy-candies 캔디	ability-abilities 능력
lady-ladies 숙녀	puppy-puppies 강아지	activity-activities 활동	history-histories 역사
vicinity-vicinities 주변	diary-diaries 일기	party-parties파티	story-stories 이야기
factory-factories 공장	body-bodies 몸	dynasty-dynasties 왕조	fairy-fairies 요정
therapy-therapies 치료법		grocery-groceries 식료품	
responsibility-responsibilities 책임			

하지만 '모음+y'로 끝나는 경우는 s만을 붙인다.

boy-boys 소년	day-days 날	way-ways 방법	toy-toys 장난감
monkey-monkeys 원숭이	holiday-holidays 국경일	journey-journeys 여행	

③ 철자가 '자음+o'로 끝날 때

potato-potatoes 감자　　tomato-tomatoes 토마토 hero-heroes 영웅

그러나 '모음+o'로 끝나는 경우는 s만을 붙인다.

radio-radios 라디오　　audio-audios 오디오　　video-videos 비디오

① 두 가지 복수명사
mosquito와 volcano는 둘 다 가능하다.

mosquito-mosquito(e)s 모기　　　　　　volcano-volcano(e)s 화산

② 축약형의 경우는 –s만 붙인다.
pianos(pianofortes) 피아노　　　　　　photos(photographs) 사진
autos(automobiles) 자동차　　　　　　solos(soloartists) 솔로가수

④ f(e)로 끝날 때, f(e)를 v로 고치고 -es를 붙인다.

knife-knives 칼　　　leaf-leaves 잎　　　life-lives 생명　　　wife-wives 아내
wolf-wolves 늑대　　　thief-thieves 도둑

① 두 가지로 쓸 수 있는 단어
scarf-scarves/scarfs 스카프　　　dwarf-dwarves/dwarfs 난장이

② 다만 축약형 등의 경우는 -s만 붙인다.
roofs(←rooftops) 지붕　　　safes(←safeguards) 금고
belief-beliefs 믿음　　　chief-chiefs 추장
proof-proofs 증거

2. 위의 ①, ②, ③, ④의 -es를 붙이는 것을 제외하면 나머지는 모두 -s를 붙인다.

book-books 책　　　week-weeks 주　　　bag-bags 가방　　　school-schools 학교
sister-sisters 누이　　　year-years 년　　　friend-friends 친구　　　month-months 달
bath-baths 목욕　　　peak-peaks 정상　　　crab-crabs 게　　　netizen-netizens 네티즌
stomach-stomachs 위　　　festival-festivals 축제　　　zebra-zebras 얼룩말
souvenir-souvenirs 기념품　　　physicist-physicists 물리학자
accountant-accountants 회계사　　　problem-problems 문제
veterinarian-veterinarians 수의사　　　computer-computers 컴퓨터

-(e)s를 붙이지 않고 복수형을 만드는 것들도 있다.

① 단수형과 복수형이 같은 것: a(n)이 붙으면 단수, 붙지 않으면 복수취급한다.
salmon-salmon 연어　　　deer-deer 사슴
sheep-sheep 양　　　Chinese-Chinese 중국인
Japanese-Japanese 일본인
fish-fish 물고기/다만 물고기의 여러 종류를 말할 때는 fishes

② 단수형의 단어의 철자가 바뀌어서 복수형이 되는 단어
mouse-mice 쥐　　　tooth-teeth 이
goose-geese 거위　　　man-men 남자
woman-women 여자　　　ox-oxen 황소
child-children 아이　　　foot-feet 발
basis- bases 기초　　　crisis-crises 위기

확인문제 1

아래 단어들의 복수형을 쓰시오.

(01). elevator –   (02). clock –

(03). branch –   (04). bush –

(05). sky –   (06). mummy –

(07). gallery –   (08). memory –

(09). knife –   (10). life –

(11). audio –   (12). stapler –

(13). heater –   (14). deer –

(15). mouse –   (16). tooth –

(17). goose –   (18). man –

(19). woman –   (20). ox –

(21). child –   (22). cashier –

(23). cook –   (24). sheep –

《정답과 해설 5P》

CF

–(e)s를 붙이는 것

–(e)s를 붙이는 것에는 두가지가 있다.

동사원형에 붙이는 것과 명사에 붙이는 것이 있고 이 두가지는 서로 완전히 다른 것이다.

① 동사원형에 –(e)s를 붙이는 것:

주어가 3인칭 단수이고 현재시제를 나타낸다.
ex)
My mother works at the bank.   나의 엄마는 은행에서 일하신다.
My grandfather teaches science.   나의 할아버지는 과학을 가르치신다.

② 명사에 –(e)s를 붙이는 것:

명사가 두개 이상이라는 뜻이다.
ex)
books, bags, foxes, buses

Grammar in Reading

〈정답과 해설 5P〉

1. 다음 (   ) 안에 알맞은 것을 넣으시오.

The rainstorm went away. I opened the window. I saw the sunlight coming through ⓐ (it, them).
I looked outside. There were no more dark ⓑ (cloud, clouds). My ⓒ (family, families) and my ⓓ
(neighbor, neighbors) were all safe.

01. ⓐ-
02. ⓑ-
03. ⓒ-
04. ⓓ-

2. 다음 (   ) 안에 알맞은 것을 넣으시오.

W: Honey, I need to fix my cellphone. The screen is broken.
M: Really? I guess it's time to change your phone.
W: I don't think so. It's only two years old.
M: Well, people change their phones every two or three years.
W: I know, but it's cheaper to replace the screen than buying a new ⓐ (phone, phones).
M: But new ⓑ (cellphone, cellphones) have a lot of good ⓒ (function, functions).
W: That's true, but I'm happy with my phone. If I fix it, I can use it for another couple of ⓓ (year,
     years).
M: I see.
W: We should try to repair things before we throw ⓔ(it, them) away.

01. ⓐ-
02. ⓑ-
03. ⓒ-
04. ⓓ-
05. ⓔ-

Grammar in Reading

〈정답과 해설 5~6P〉

3. 다음 (   ) 안에 알맞은 것을 넣으시오.

ⓐ (A dog, Dogs) have helped blind ⓑ (people, peoples) for many ⓒ (year, years). But they are not the only helper animals. There are also ⓓ (guide horse, guide horses). They can help blind people to get where they want to go. They are better than dogs for people who do not want to keep their guide animals in the house. Plus, they live a lot longer than dogs. They can live up to 40 ⓔ (year, years).

01. ⓐ-
02. ⓑ-
03. ⓒ-
04. ⓓ-
05. ⓔ-

4. 다음 (   ) 안에 알맞은 것을 넣으시오.

M: This play ⓐ (room, rooms) looks great, Ms. Johnson.
W: Thanks. I put a boat in the corner since ⓑ (a child, children) love boats.
M: It was a great idea to put a ladder on the side of the boat.
W: Children can climb on it. I also drew two ⓒ (fish, fishes) on the floor.
M: Excellent. Is that a light house on the wall?
W: Yeah. It will help ⓓ (a child, children) imagine they're at sea.
M: That's perfect. And I like that table as well.
W: I'm glad you like it. For the kids' safety, I chose a round table instead of a square one.
M: Brilliant! What are these ⓔ (box, boxes) for? Their sizes are all different.
W: They can be used for sitting, stepping on and playing with.
M: Good. I'm sure children will love this place.

01. ⓐ-
02. ⓑ-
03. ⓒ-
04. ⓓ-
05. ⓔ-

〈정답과 해설 6P〉

1. 다음 명사의 복수형을 쓰시오.

01. month –   02. glass –

03. fox –   04. thief –

05. friend –   06. man –

07. sandwich –   08. computer –

09. box –   10. bus –

11. church –   12. desk –

13. bench –   14. match –

15. wish –   16. address –

17. brush –   18. watch –

19. blouse –   20. house –

2. 다음 명사의 복수형을 쓰시오.

01. piece –   02. potato –

03. tomato –   04. wife –

05. piano –   06. photo –

07. auto –   08. solo –

09. radio –   10. audio –

〈정답과 해설 6P〉

11. video –   12. zoo –

13. family –   14. baby –

15. ox –   16. city –

17. book –   18. country –

19. candy –   20. day –

3. 다음 명사의 복수형을 쓰시오.

01. party –   02. toy –

03. story –   04. woman –

05. factory –   06. lady –

07. week –   08. diary –

09. body –   10. boy –

11. monkey –   12. holiday –

13. bath –   14. problem –

15. knife –   16. leaf –

17. bag –   18. life –

19. wolf –   20. hero –

중간 · 기말고사 내신만점대비문제

〈정답과 해설 6P〉

4. 다음 명사의 복수형을 쓰시오.

01. school –

02. roof –

03. safe –

04. sheep –

05. salmon –

06. sister –

07. tooth –

08. deer –

09. fish –

10. year –

11. goose –

12. foot –

13. mouse –

14. computer –

15. train –

16. smart phone –

17. electrician –

18. journalist –

19. official –

20. statesman –

5. 다음 명사의 복수형을 쓰시오.

01. designer –

02. engineer –

03. manager –

04. author –

05. editor –

06. minister –

07. pilot –

08. salesperson –

09. reporter –

10. manicurist –

〈정답과 해설 6~7P〉

11. lawyer –

12. soldier –

13. receptionist –

14. physical therapist –

15. locksmith –

16. security guard –

17. veterinarian –

18. photographer –

19. stockbroker –

20. century –

6. 다음 괄호 안에서 알맞은 형태를 고르시오.

01. The boys are (a student, students).

02. (Mice, Mouse) are small animals.

03. The (pineapple, pineapples) is in the basket.

04. These are Mark's (a book, books).

05. Those (scissor, scissors) cut well.

06. The (roofs, rooves) of the museum are green.

07. Many (leafs, leaves) are falling from the tree.

08. Some (childs, children) are making snowmen outside.

09. There are many (deer, deers) in the grass.

10. The businessman bought some (kind, kinds) of smart books in the market.

〈정답과 해설 7P〉

7. 다음 문장에서 어법상 어색한 부분을 찾아 바르게 고쳐 쓰시오.

01. I brush my tooth three times a day.
_____ → _____

02. There are many deers in the forest.
_____ → _____

03. The boy wants to buy a pair of pant.
_____ → _____

04. There are many kinds of piano in the shop.
_____ → _____

05. There are some bench in the park.
_____ → _____

06. There are a lot of fish in the river.
_____ → _____

07. They grow a lot of tomato in their greenhouse.
_____ → _____

08. She put five fork and five knife on the table.
_____ → _____, _____ → _____

09. He has ten goose on his farm.
_____ → _____

10. Two woman are looking at the lizard.
_____ → _____

〈정답과 해설 7P〉

8. 다음 문장에서 어법상 어색한 부분을 찾아 바르게 고쳐 쓰시오.(2개인 경우도 있음)

01. He has two babys.

02. She caught a lot of fishes.

03. There are three wolfs in the zoo.

04. Many child are on the street.

05. I'll buy a few apple pies for you.

06. How much times have you met the actor?

07. I have two sister and three brother.

08. I'll give some sandwiches to your sister.

09. How many ball is there in the basket?

10. There are a computer and two picture in my room.

11. There are hundreds of people in the concert hall.

12. A lot of sheeps browses and play in the meadow.

Chapter

03

Making verbs into Past & Past Participle
과거, 과거분사 만들기

‖ 규칙동사의 과거, 과거분사(p.p)형 만들기

규칙동사의 과거, 과거분사(p.p)형 만들기

일반적으로 동사원형에 –(e)d를 붙인다.

동사원형 + ed	아래 특별한 경우를 제외하고 대부분의 경우	play – played – played watch – watched – watched happen – happened – happened
특별한 경우	–e 로 끝나는 경우: –d만 붙인다.	decide – decided – decided dance – danced – danced save – saved–saved
	자음+y로 끝날 때: y를 i로 고치고–ed를 붙인다. 다만 모음+y일 때는 그냥 –ed만 붙인다.	study – studied – studied marry – married – married cf> '모음+y'는 –ed만 붙인다. play – played – played
	1음절단어와 뒤에 엑센트 오는 2음절 단어의 발음이 [단모음]+[단자음]일 때 마지막 자음을 더 쓰고 –ed cf> 다만 2음절 단어가 앞에 엑센트 있을 때는 그냥 –ed만 붙인다.	shop – shopped – shopped drop – dropped – dropped combát – combatted – combatted commít – committed – committed cf> 액센트가 1음절에 있는 경우 énter – entered – entered vísit – visited – visited

1. 동사원형ed

- add – added – added   보태다
- shout – shouted – shouted   소리치다
- invent – invented – invented   발명하다
- walk – walked – walked   걷다

- look – looked – looked   보다
- ask – asked – asked   묻다
- kick – kicked – kicked   차다
- talk – talked – talked   말하다
- watch – watched – watched   보다
- jump – jumped – jumped   점프하다
- rain – rained – rained   비가 내리다
- explain – explained – explained   설명하다
- show – showed – showed   보여주다
- answer – answered – answered   대답하다
- arrive – arrived – arrived   도착하다
- harm – harmed – harmed   해를 끼치다
- spell – spelled – spelled   스펠링을 쓰다
- spoil – spoiled – spoiled   망치다
- happen – happened – happened   일어나다

2. 특별한 경우

① –e로 끝나는 경우: –d만 붙인다.
- like – liked – liked   좋아하다
- move – moved – moved   움직이다
- close – closed – closed   막다
- decide – decided – decided   결정하다
- save – saved – saved   저축하다

② 자음+y로 끝나는 경우: –y를 i로 고치고 ed를 붙인다.
- try – tried – tried   노력하다
- cry – cried – cried   울다
- carry – carried – carried   운반하다
- worry – worried – worried   걱정하다
- hurry – hurried – hurried   서두르다
- marry – married – married   결혼하다
- study – studied – studied   공부하다

다만 모음+y인 경우는 그냥 -ed만 붙인다.

- stay – stayed – stayed   머무르다
- obey – obeyed – obeyed   복종하다
- enjoy – enjoyed – enjoyed   즐기다

③ 단모음+단자음으로 끝나는 경우: 마지막 자음을 하나 겹치고 -ed를 붙인다.

1음절어

- stop – stopped – stopped 멈추다

2음절– 뒤에 액센트가 오는 단어

- occúr – occurred – occurred 발생하다
- admít – admitted – admitted 인정하다

 확인문제 1

다음 단어들의 과거형과 p.p(과거분사)을 쓰시오. 그리고 단어의 뜻을 쓰시오.

(01). shout   _____, _____, _____

(02). explain   _____, _____, _____

(03). remind   _____, _____, _____

(04). threaten   _____, _____, _____

(05). climb   _____, _____, _____

(06). drop   _____, _____, _____

(07). find   _____, _____, _____

(08). found   _____, _____, _____

(09). fail   _____, _____, _____

(10). disappear   _____, _____, _____

(11). succeed   _____, _____, _____

(12). happen   _____, _____, _____

(13). raise   _____, _____, _____

(14). pick   _____, _____, _____

(15). decide   _____, _____, _____

(16). provide   _____, _____, _____

(17). offer   _____, _____, _____

(18). allow   _____, _____, _____

(19). excuse   _____, _____, _____

(20). accept   _____, _____, _____

〈정답과 해설 7P〉

확인문제 2

다음 단어들의 과거형과 p.p(과거분사)을 쓰시오. 그리고 단어의 뜻을 쓰시오.

(01). receive _____, _____, _____

(02). mix _____, _____, _____

(03). gather _____, _____, _____

(04). compare _____, _____, _____

(05). fill _____, _____, _____

(06). supply _____, _____, _____

(07). stay _____, _____, _____

(08). clean _____, _____, _____

(09. vary _____, _____, _____

(10). cry _____, _____, _____

(11). visit _____, _____, _____

(12). classify _____, _____, _____

(13). bury _____, _____, _____

(14). apply _____, _____, _____

(15). spray _____, _____, _____

(16). commit _____, _____, _____

(17). chat _____, _____, _____

(18). stop _____, _____, _____

(19). grab _____, _____, _____

(20). enter _____, _____, _____

〈정답과 해설 7P〉

확인문제 3

다음 단어들의 과거형과 p.p(과거분사)을 쓰시오. 그리고 단어의 뜻을 쓰시오.

(01). waste _____, _____, _____

(02). spend _____, _____, _____

(03). use _____, _____, _____

(04). collect _____, _____, _____

(05). shape _____, _____, _____

(06). prepare _____, _____, _____

(07). found _____, _____, _____

(08). form _____, _____, _____

(09). develop _____ , _____ , _____

(10). refuse _____ , _____ , _____

(11). store _____ , _____ , _____

(12). prevent _____ , _____ , _____

(13). limit _____ , _____ , _____

(14). save _____ , _____ , _____

(15). pull _____ , _____ , _____

(16). continue _____ , _____ , _____

(17). join _____ , _____ , _____

(18). rest _____ , _____ , _____

(19). settle _____ , _____ , _____

(20). serve _____ , _____ , _____

〈정답과 해설 8P〉

-ed형태의 발음

A. [id]로 발음 하는 것- 단어 끝 발음이 [t]나 [d]로 발음 나는 것

end – ended – ended	끝나다
want – wanted – wanted	원하다
mend – mended – mended	수리하다
visit – visited – visited	방문하다
admit – admitted – admitted	인정하다

B. [t]로 발음 되는 것

단어 끝 발음이 [t]를 제외한 무성음 [k, p , f, s, θ, ∫, ʧ]이 올 때

work – worked – worked	일하다
help – helped – helped	돕다
laugh – laughed – laughed	웃다
miss – missed – missed	놓치다
wish – wished – wished	소망하다
touch – touched – touched	터치하다
push – pushed – pushed	밀다
stop – stopped – stopped	멈추다

[d]로 발음되는 것
[d]음을 제외한 유성자음[v, g, b, z, ʒ, ʤ, l, m, n, r]등과 모든 모음발음[a, ɔ, ə, ʌ, i, æ]으로 끝나는 단어.

stay – stayed – stayed	머무르다
live – lived – lived	살다
learn – learned – learned	배우다
open – opened – opened	열다
clean – cleaned – cleaned	청소하다
call – called – called	부르다
cheer – cheered – cheered	응원하다
raise – raised – raised	올리다
judge – judged – judged	판단하다
enjoy – enjoyed – enjoyed	즐기다
play – played – played	놀다
move – moved – moved	움직이다
close – closed – closed	닫다
marry – married – married	결혼하다
study – studied – studied	공부하다

 확인문제 4

다음 동사의 과거형과 p.p(과거분사)형의 –ed 발음이 [id], [t], [d] 중 어느 것으로 발음되는 지를 각각 말하시오.

(01).enjoyed _____	(02). played _____	(03). helped _____
(04) laughed _____	(05). moved _____	(06). ended _____
(07). wanted _____	(08). mended _____	(09). closed _____
(10). missed _____	(11). studied _____	(12). visited _____
(13). liked _____	(14). admited _____	(15). worked _____
(16). touched _____	(17). cleaned _____	(18). called _____
(19). cheered _____	(20). raised _____	(21). judged _____
(22). pushed _____	(23). started _____	(24). stopped _____
(25). stayed _____	(26). lived _____	(27). wished _____
(28). married _____	(29). learned _____	(30). opened _____

〈정답과 해설 8P〉

Grammar in Reading

〈정답과 해설 8P〉

1. 다음 괄호 안에 과거형동사를 어법에 맞추어 쓰시오.

Javlon is a 14-year-old boy who ⓐ(be) born and ⓑ(grow) up in Uzbekistan. His father ⓒ(get) a new job in Korea, so his family ⓓ(move) to Seoul three months ago. He ⓔ(start) to write about Korea on the Internet.

Let's look at the writings that Javlon ⓕ(post) on his blog.

01. ⓐ _____   02. ⓑ _____
03. ⓒ _____   04. ⓓ _____
05. ⓔ _____   06. ⓕ _____

2. 다음 괄호 안에 현재형동사를 어법에 맞추어 쓰시오.

Today was my first day at school. School life ⓐ(be) a little different here in Korea. Back in Uzbekistan, school ⓑ(begin) in fall. In Korea, school ⓒ(start) in spring. When students ⓓ(see) teachers, they ⓔ(bow) to them. Isn't that strange? Also, students here don't call older students just by their first names. They ⓕ(think) it is rude.

I hope I learn Korean culture quickly.

01. ⓐ _____   02. ⓑ _____
03. ⓒ _____   04. ⓓ _____
05. ⓔ _____   06. ⓕ _____

Grammar in Reading

〈정답과 해설 8P〉

3. 다음 괄호 안에 과거형동사를 어법에 맞추어 쓰시오.

After school, Jihun ⓐ(ask) me to play soccer with him and his friends. I often ⓑ(play) soccer in Uzbekistan, so I ⓒ(join) them right away. I ⓓ(score) two goals and my team ⓔ(win) the game by one goal! Jihun ⓕ(be) proud of me.

I ⓖ(be) also very proud of myself. Jihun ⓗ(ask) me to join his soccer club and I ⓘ(say), "Yes, of course!"

01. ⓐ _____	02. ⓑ _____
03. ⓒ _____	04. ⓓ _____
05. ⓔ _____	06. ⓕ _____
07. ⓖ _____	08. ⓗ _____
09. ⓘ _____	

Grammar in Reading

〈정답과 해설 9P〉

4. 다음 괄호 안에 과거형동사를 어법에 맞추어 쓰시오.

Today ⓐ(be) Navruz, the New Year holiday in Uzbekistan. I ⓑ(invite) Jihun and some Korean friends to my house, and we ⓒ(celebrate) the holiday together. I ⓓ(show) them some pictures of activities on Navruz.

My mom ⓔ(cook) us Sumalak, an Uzbekistani food. My friends ⓕ(like) its sweet taste, but my mom ⓖ(say) there ⓗ(be) no sugar in it.
The secret is the angels' magic touch. They come down at night, and like magic, it becomes sweet and delicious. How interesting! Jihun and other friends ⓘ(tell) me that they would like to invite me on Korean holidays.
I want to know more about Korean holidays.

01. ⓐ _____   02. ⓑ _____
03. ⓒ _____   04. ⓓ _____
05. ⓔ _____   06. ⓕ _____
07. ⓖ _____   08. ⓗ _____
09. ⓘ _____

5. 다음 (   ) 안의 주어진 단어를 이용하여 빈칸을 알맞게 채우시오.

In 1969, two boys ⓐ (see) a baby lion in a cage in a department store in London. They ⓑ (decide) to buy it and ⓒ (call) it Christian. They ⓓ (love) him very much. After a few years, he ⓔ (become) too big for their house, and they ⓕ (decide) to send him to a wildlife park in Africa. After a year, they wanted to visit Christian, but people ⓖ (say) that he would not recognize them. When they ⓗ (get) there, however, Christian recognized them. He ⓘ (run) up and ⓙ (hug) them.

01. ⓐ _____   02. ⓑ _____
03. ⓒ _____   04. ⓓ _____
05. ⓔ _____   06. ⓕ _____
07. ⓖ _____   08. ⓗ _____
09. ⓘ _____   10. ⓙ _____

〈정답과 해설 9P〉

1. 다음 문장의 (   )안에 동사를 과거동사로 쓰시오.

01. We (   ) more plastic.(recycle)

02. Everyone (   ) at that.(laugh)

03. School (   ) at five.(close)

04. The soup (   ) sweet.(smell)

05. The thief (   ) shortly.(answer)

06. Boys (   ) in the road.(dance)

07. The lion (   ) exhausted.(look)

08. I (   ) her cook dinner.(help)

09. The fox (   ) very curious.(seem)

10. She (   ) about her weight.(worry)

2. 다음 문장의 (   )의 동사를 과거동사로 쓰시오.

01. They (   ) more solar energy.(use)

02. The queen (   ) the singer.(marry)

03. The president (   ) to the people.(lie)

04. The travellers (   ) to the bus stop.(hurry)

05. To his surprise, Serena (   ) for joy.(cry)

06. His brother (　　　　) him a question.(ask)

07. The little prince (　　　　) politely.(respond)

08. The fisher (　　　　) his son to be a pilot.(expect)

09. 90 percent of all species (　　　　).(disappear)

10. The boys (　　　　) a little surprised.(look)

11. The merchant (　　　　) that he could do it.(hope)

12. The teacher (　　　　) me to clean the blackboard.(ask)

13. The manager (　　　　) a vacation with his family.(plan)

14. We (　　　　) it difficult to master English in three years.(believe)

15. Two and a half centuries ago only a few people (　　　　).(travel)

3. 다음문장의 (　　　　) 안에 p.p(과거분사)를 쓰시오.

01. They have (recycle) more plastic.

02. Everyone has (laugh) at his action.

03. The elementary School has (close) up to today.

04. The fish soup has (smell) sweet.

05. The thieves have never (answer) the questions.

06. Boys have (dance) in the road for three hours.

〈정답과 해설 8P〉

07. The lion has (look) exhausted since noon.

08. The man has (help) his wife cook dinner.

09. The foxes have (seem) very curious.

10. The fashion model has (worry) about her weight.

4. 다음 문장의 (   ) 안에 주어진 동사의 알맞은 형태를 쓰시오.

01. The villagers have (use) more solar energy.

02. The king have (know) the singer.

03. The president have (lie) to the people for 5 years.

04. The travellers have (go) to the bus stop.

05. To his surprise, Serena have (cry) for joy for an hour.

06. His dad has (ask) him questions since 5th grade .

07. The little prince has (respond) politely to the princess.

08. The fisher has (expect) his son to be a pilot for 20 years.

09. 90 percent of all species has (disappear) up to now.

10. The boys have (look) a little surprised since yesterday.

11. The merchant has (hope) that he can do it.

12. The teacher has (ask) me to clean the blackboard.

〈정답과 해설 8P〉

13. The manager has (plan) a vacation with his family.

14. We have (believe) it difficult to master English in three years.

15. For a quarter century only a few people have (travel).

Chapter

04

Irregular Verbs
불규칙 동사의 동사변화형

‖ 과거, 과거분사(p.p)형이 불규칙한 동사들

불규칙적으로 변화는 동사의 과거형과 과거분사(p.p)형

동사의 과거형과 과거분사(p,p)형이 불규칙하게 변화하는 단어들도 있다.

1. A – A – A형

의미	원형	과거형	p.p(과거분사)
터지다, 파열하다	burst	burst	burst
던지다	cast	cast	cast
비용이 들다	cost	cost	cost
자르다	cut	cut	cut
차다, 때리다	hit	hit	hit
상처를 입히다	hurt	hurt	hurt
허락하다	let	let	let
놓다	put	put	put
두다	set	set	set
흘리다	shed	shed	shed
닫다	shut	shut	shut
퍼지다	spread	spread	spread
찌르다	thrust	thrust	thrust
뒤엎다	upset	upset	upset
읽다	read	read	read
때리다,패배시키다	beat	beat	beaten/beat

2. A – B – A형

의미	원형	과거형	p.p(과거분사)
～이 되다	become	became	become
오다	come	came	come
달리다	run	ran	run
극복하다	overcome	overcame	overcome

확인문제 1

다음 동사의 과거형과 p.p(과거분사)형을 각각 쓰시오.

(01). 터지다, 파열하다.　burst　＿＿＿＿＿＿, ＿＿＿＿＿＿

(02). 던지다　cast　＿＿＿＿＿＿, ＿＿＿＿＿＿

(03). 때리다, 패배시키다　beat　＿＿＿＿＿＿, ＿＿＿＿＿＿

(04). 달리다　run　＿＿＿＿＿＿, ＿＿＿＿＿＿

(05). 비용이 들다　cost　＿＿＿＿＿＿, ＿＿＿＿＿＿

(06). 치다, 때리다　hit　＿＿＿＿＿＿, ＿＿＿＿＿＿

(07). 고르다　choose　＿＿＿＿＿＿, ＿＿＿＿＿＿

(08). 허락하다　let　＿＿＿＿＿＿, ＿＿＿＿＿＿

(09). ～되다.　become　＿＿＿＿＿＿, ＿＿＿＿＿＿

(10). 이끌다　lead　＿＿＿＿＿＿, ＿＿＿＿＿＿

(11). 두다　set　＿＿＿＿＿＿, ＿＿＿＿＿＿

(12). 오다　come　＿＿＿＿＿＿, ＿＿＿＿＿＿

(13). 노래하다　sing　＿＿＿＿＿＿, ＿＿＿＿＿＿

(14). 지불하다　pay　＿＿＿＿＿＿, ＿＿＿＿＿＿

(15). 흘리다　shed　＿＿＿＿＿＿, ＿＿＿＿＿＿

(16). 찌르다　thrust　＿＿＿＿＿＿, ＿＿＿＿＿＿

(17). 흔들다　swing　＿＿＿＿＿＿, ＿＿＿＿＿＿

(18). 수영하다　swim　＿＿＿＿＿＿, ＿＿＿＿＿＿

(19). 뒤엎다　upset　＿＿＿＿＿＿, ＿＿＿＿＿＿

(20). 퍼지다　spread　＿＿＿＿＿＿, ＿＿＿＿＿＿

〈정답과 해설 10P〉

3. A -B- B형

의미	원형	과거형	p.p(과거분사)
구부리다	bend	bent	bent
가져오다	bring	brought	brought
사다	buy	bought	bought
잡다	catch	caught	caught
기다	creep	crept	crept
다루다	deal	dealt	dealt
파다	dig	dug	dug
거주하다, 살다	dwell	dwelt/dwelled	dwelt/dwelled
먹이를 주다	feed	fed	fed
느끼다	feel	felt	felt
싸우다	fight	fought	fought
듣다	hear	heard	heard
잡다, 손에 들다	hold	held	held
지키다	keep	kept	kept
이끌다	lead	led	led
떠나다	leave	left	left
빌려주다	lend	lent	lent
잃다	lose	lost	lost
의미하다	mean	meant	meant
만나다	meet	met	met
지불하다	pay	paid	paid
말하다	say	said	said
찾다, 구하다	seek	sought	sought
팔다	sell	sold	sold
빛나다	shine	shone	shone
쏘다	shoot	shot	shot
잠자다	sleep	slept	slept
소비하다	spend	spent	spent

의미	원형	과거형	p.p(과거분사)
돌다, 잣다	spin	spun	spun
서다	stand	stood	stood
찌르다, 고수하다	stick	stuck	stuck
치다	strike	struck	struck
청소하다	sweep	swept	swept
흔들다	swing	swung	swung
가르치다	teach	taught	taught
생각하다	think	thought	thought
울다	weep	wept	wept
이기다	win	won	won

🔍 확인문제 2

다음 동사의 과거형과 p.p(과거분사)형을 각각 쓰시오.

(01). 구부리다   bend   _____ , _____

(02). 가져오다   bring   _____ , _____

(03). 사다   buy   _____ , _____

(04). 잡다   catch   _____ , _____

(05). 기다   creep   _____ , _____

(06). 다루다   deal   _____ , _____

(07). 파다   dig   _____ , _____

(08). 거주하다, 살다   dwell   _____ , _____

(09). 먹이를 주다   feed   _____ , _____

(10). 느끼다   feel   _____ , _____

(11). 싸우다   fight   _____ , _____

(12). 듣다   hear   _____ , _____

(13). 잡다   hold   _____ , _____

(14). 지키다   keep   _____ , _____

(15). 이끌다   lead   _____ , _____

(16). 떠나다   leave   _____ , _____

(17). 빌려주다   lend   _____ , _____

(18). 잃다   lose   _____ , _____

(19). 의미하다   mean   _____ , _____

(20). 만나다	meet	_____ ,	_____
(21). 지불하다	pay	_____ ,	_____
(22). 말하다	say	_____ ,	_____
(23). 찾다, 구하다	seek	_____ ,	_____
(24). 팔다	sell	_____ ,	_____
(25). 빛나다	shine	_____ ,	_____
(26). 쏘다	shoot	_____ ,	_____
(27). 잠자다	sleep	_____ ,	_____
(28). 소비하다	spend	_____ ,	_____
(29). 잣다	spin	_____ ,	_____
(30). 서다	stand	_____ ,	_____
(31). 찌르다, 고수하다	stick	_____ ,	_____
(32). 치다	strike	_____ ,	_____
(33). 청소하다	sweep	_____ ,	_____
(34). 흔들다	swing	_____ ,	_____
(35). 가르치다	teach	_____ ,	_____
(36). 생각하다	think	_____ ,	_____
(37). 울다	weep	_____ ,	_____
(38). 이기다	win	_____ ,	_____

〈정답과 해설 10P〉

4. A - B - C형

의미	원형	과거형	p.p(과거분사)
시작하다	begin	began	begun
물다	bite	bit	bitten/bit
불다	blow	blew	blown
부수다	break	broke	broken
고르다	choose	chose	chosen
그리다, 끌다	draw	drew	drawn
마시다	drink	drank	drunk
운전하다	drive	drove	driven
먹다	eat	ate	eaten

의미	원형	과거형	p.p(과거분사)
날다	fly	flew	flown
잊다	forget	forgot	forgot/forgotten
성장하다	grow	grew	grown
숨기다	hide	hid	hidden
알다	know	knew	known
타다	ride	rode	ridden
울리다	ring	rang	rung
오르다	rise	rose	risen
흔들다	shake	shook	shaken
보여주다	show	showed	showed/shown
노래하다	sing	sang	sung
가라앉다	sink	sank	sunk
말하다	speak	spoke	spoken
훔치다	steal	stole	stolen
노력하다	strive	strove	striven
맹세하다	swear	swore	sworn
수영하다	swim	swam	swum
찢다	tear	tore	torn
던지다	throw	threw	thrown
입다	wear	wore	worn
쓰다	write	wrote	written

다음 동사의 과거형과 p.p(과거분사)형을 각각 쓰시오. 그리고 뜻을 쓰시오,

(01). begin   _____,   _____,   _____

(02). read   _____,   _____,   _____

(03). bite   _____,   _____,   _____

(04). blow   _____,   _____,   _____

(05). break   _____,   _____,   _____

(06). cut   _____,   _____,   _____

(07). draw   _____,   _____,   _____

(08). drink   _____,   _____,   _____

(09). drive   _____,   _____,   _____

(10). eat   _____,   _____,   _____

(11). fly   _____,   _____,   _____

(12).forget   _____,   _____,   _____

(13). apply   _____,   _____,   _____

(14). grow   _____,   _____,   _____

(15). hide   _____,   _____,   _____

(16). hurt   _____,   _____,   _____

(17). know   _____,   _____,   _____

(18). ride   _____,   _____,   _____

(19). put   _____,   _____,   _____

(20). ring   _____,   _____,   _____

(21). rise   _____,   _____,   _____

(22). shake   _____,   _____,   _____

(23). show   _____,   _____,   _____

(24). sink   _____,   _____,   _____

(25). speak   _____,   _____,   _____

(26). steal   _____,   _____,   _____

(27). strive   _____,   _____,   _____

(28). swear   _____,   _____,   _____

(29). tear   _____,   _____,   _____

(30). throw   _____,   _____,   _____

(31). wear   _____,   _____,   _____

(32). write   _____,   _____,   _____

〈정답과 해설 10P〉

5. 뜻에 따라 활용이 달라지는 불규칙 동사

원형	의미	과거형	p.p(과거분사)
bear	참다	bore	borne
	낳다	bore	born
bid	명령하다, 말하다	bade	bidden
	값을 매기다	bid	bid
hang	걸다	hung	hung
	교수형에 처하다	hanged	hanged
lie	눕다	lay	lain
	거짓말하다	lied	lied

🔍 확인문제 4

다음 동사의 과거형과 p.p(과거분사)형을 각각 쓰시오.

(01). bear ┌ 낳다 ⓐ _____, _____
       └ 참다 ⓑ _____, _____

(02). bid ┌ 값을 매기다 ⓐ _____, _____
      └ 명령하다, 말하다 ⓑ _____, _____

(03). hang ┌ 교수형에 처하다 ⓐ _____, _____
       └ 걸다 ⓑ _____, _____

(04). lie ┌ 거짓말하다 ⓐ _____, _____
      └ 눕다 ⓑ _____, _____

〈정답과 해설 10P〉

6. 혼동하기 쉬운 불규칙동사

의미	원형	과거형	p.p(과거분사)
묶다	bind	bound	bound
되튀다	bound	bounded	bounded
떨어지다, 쓰러지다	fall	fell	fallen
쓰러뜨리다	fell	felled	felled
발견하다	find	found	found
세우다, 창립하다	found	founded	founded
날다	fly	flew	flown
흐르다	flow	flowed	flowed
눕다	lie	lay	lain
~를 놓다, 눕히다	lay	laid	laid
보다	see	saw	seen
톱질하다	saw	sawed	sawed/sawn
앉다	sit	sat	sat
두다	set	set	set
감다	wind	wound	wound
상처를 입히다	wound	wounded	wounded
환영하다	welcome	welcomed	welcomed
이겨내다, 극복하다	overcome	overcame	overcome

다음 동사의 과거형과 p.p(과거분사)형을 각각 쓰시오. 그리고 뜻을 쓰시오.

(01). bind   _____ ,   _____ ,   _____

(02). bound   _____ ,   _____ ,   _____

(03). fall   _____ ,   _____ ,   _____

(04). fell   _____ ,   _____ ,   _____

(05). find   _____ ,   _____ ,   _____

(06). found   _____ ,   _____ ,   _____

(07). fly   _____ ,   _____ ,   _____

(08). flow   _____ ,   _____ ,   _____

(09). lie   ⓐ _____ ,   _____ ,   거짓말하다.

             ⓑ _____ ,   _____ ,   눕다, 놓여있다.

(10). lay   _____ ,   _____ ,   _____

(11). see   _____ ,   _____ ,   _____

(12). saw   _____ ,   _____ ,   _____

(13). sit   _____ ,   _____ ,   _____

(14). set   _____ ,   _____ ,   _____

(15). wind   _____ ,   _____ ,   _____

(16). wound   _____ ,   _____ ,   _____

(17). welcome _____ ,   _____ ,   _____

(18). overcome _____ ,   _____ ,   _____

〈정답과 해설 10P〉

중간 · 기말고사 내신만점대비문제

〈정답과 해설 11P〉

1. 다음 동사의 3인칭 단수 현재형과 과거형, 그리고 'p.p-과거분사형'을 쓰시오. 그리고 뜻을 쓰시오.

01. abandon   _____,   _____,   _____,   _____

02. allow   _____,   _____,   _____,   _____

03. ask   _____,   _____,   _____,   _____

04. avoid   _____,   _____,   _____,   _____

05. advise   _____,   _____,   _____,   _____

06. be   _____,   _____,   _____,   _____

07. chat   _____,   _____,   _____,   _____

08. clap   _____,   _____,   _____,   _____

09. do   _____,   _____,   _____,   _____

10. put   _____,   _____,   _____,   _____

11. set   _____,   _____,   _____,   _____

12. hit   _____,   _____,   _____,   _____

13. burst   _____,   _____,   _____,   _____

14. cast   _____,   _____,   _____,   _____

15. cut   _____,   _____,   _____,   _____

16. command   _____,   _____,   _____,   _____

17. cause   _____,   _____,   _____,   _____

18. compel   _____,   _____,   _____,   _____

19. desire   _____,   _____,   _____,   _____

20. demand   _____,   _____,   _____,   _____

2. 다음 동사의 3인칭 단수 현재형과 과거형, 그리고 p.p-과거분사형을 쓰시오. 단어의 뜻도 쓰시오.

01. deny   _____,   _____,   _____,   _____

02. encourage   _____,   _____,   _____,   _____

03. expect   _____,   _____,   _____,   _____

04. enable   _____,   _____,   _____,   _____

05. read   _____,   _____,   _____,   _____

06. lead   _____,   _____,   _____,   _____

07. shut   _____,   _____,   _____,   _____

08. cast   _____,   _____,   _____,   _____

09. mix   _____,   _____,   _____,   _____

10. lock   _____,   _____,   _____,   _____

11. imagine   _____,   _____,   _____,   _____

12. suppose   _____,   _____,   _____,   _____

13. finish   _____,   _____,   _____,   _____

14. feel   _____,   _____,   _____,   _____

15. forbid   _____,   _____,   _____,   _____

〈정답과 해설 11P〉

16. force   _____, _____, _____, _____

17. guess   _____, _____, _____, _____

18. think   _____, _____, _____, _____

19. know   _____, _____, _____, _____

20. agree   _____, _____, _____, _____

3. 다음 동사의 3인칭 단수 현재형과 과거형, 그리고 p.p-과거분사형을 쓰시오. 단어의 뜻을 쓰시오.

01. breathe   _____, _____, _____, _____

02. apply   _____, _____, _____, _____

03. classify   _____, _____, _____, _____

04. cry   _____, _____, _____, _____

05. fly   _____, _____, _____, _____

06. fry   _____, _____, _____, _____

07. enjoy   _____, _____, _____, _____

08. stay   _____, _____, _____, _____

09. play   _____, _____, _____, _____

10. copy   _____, _____, _____, _____

11. relax   _____, _____, _____, _____

〈정답과 해설 11P〉

12. wash   _____,   _____,   _____,   _____

13. pass   _____,   _____,   _____,   _____

14. teach   _____,   _____,   _____,   _____

15. say   _____,   _____,   _____,   _____

16. surf   _____,   _____,   _____,   _____

17. leave   _____,   _____,   _____,   _____

18. grow   _____,   _____,   _____,   _____

4. 다음 문장에서 틀린 것을 찾아 올바로 고치시오.

01. Mac didn't made robots yesterday.

02. They did helped the poor children last month.

03.
  A: Do you have a nice trip during your vacation?
  B: Yes, I did. It was great.

04.
  A: What did you do yesterday?
  B: I take computer lessons.

05.
  A: Where did you go during the vacation?
  B: I go to an art camp. It was great.

〈정답과 해설 11P〉

5. 다음 빈칸에 과거형 동사를 쓰시오,

01. His grandfather _____ two years ago.(die)

02. She _____ the dishes yesterday.(wash)

03. Sam _____ loudly last night.(sing)

04. The movie _____ an hour ago. (start)

05. John _____ some comic books yesterday.(read)

06. The tiger _____ grass an hour ago.(eat)

07. Jane _____ to school by bus yesterday.(go)

08. He _____ photographs last weekend.(take)

09. I _____ the work at 7 o'clock last night.(finish)

10. Some birds _____ in the sky last summer.(fly)

11. They _____ their uncle's house last Saturday. (visit)

12. Kevin and I _____ to the library last Friday. (go)

13. My grandma _____ to my birthday party three days ago.(come)

14. She _____ Chris at Amy's birthday party yesterday.(meet)

15. My grandfather _____ this house twenty years old. (build)

16. Yesterday was Minho's birthday. We _____ a book for him. (buy)

17. Her parents _____ a puppy to their son last birthday.(give)

18. The taxi driver (   ) a car carefully and slowly.(drive)

〈정답과 해설 12P〉

19. He (   ) it convenient to use a vacuum cleaner.(think)

20. The refugees (   ) up to find themselves bloody and hurt.(wake)

6. 다음 문장의 (   ) 안에 과거동사를 쓰시오.

01. Clara (   ) married.(get)

02. His room (   ) clean.(keep)

03. A man (   ) the driver.(hurt)

04. The boys (   ) to the school.(run)

05. Their dream (   ) true.(come)

06. Girls (   ) such books.(read)

07. An earthquake (   ) again.(begin)

08. The sun (   ) brightly.(shine)

09. The rumor (   ) quickly.(spread)

10. My master (   ) so guilty.(feel)

11. His father (   ) him a book. (buy)

12. My father (   ) me happy.(make)

13. My mom (   ) the box safe.(keep)

14. The wind (   ) heavily.(blow)

15. The river (   ) last night.(freeze)

〈정답과 해설 12P〉

16. The sun (   ) in the east.(rise)

17. The dancers (   ) in the stage.(sing)

18. The teacher (   ) us science.(teach)

19. The merchant (   ) fish.(buy)

20. The bomb (   ) immediately.(burst)

7. 다음 문장의 (   ) 안에 과거동사를 쓰시오.

01. His sister (   ) a best pianist.(become)

02. The merchant (   ) me a letter.(send)

03. Soldier (   ) a gun to the citizens.(shoot)

04. The babies (   ) in the armchair.(sleep)

05. The farmer (   ) his baby sleeping.(see)

06. The worker (   ) on the escalator.(fall)

07. They also (   ) me beautiful flowers.(send)

08. The two boys (   ) the wall dirty.(make)

09. David (   ) me to water the plant.(want)

10. The cat (   ) the bird go free. (let)

11. The fire (   ) an elderly woman dead.(leave)

12. The child (   ) his promise.(forget)

〈정답과 해설 12P〉

13. The singer (   ) on the stage.(stand)

14. People (   ) that she had married.(know)

15. The whole building (   ) a little.(shake)

16. My friend (   ) me a smart phone.(choose)

17. You (   ) Mary plant those trees.(see)

18. Oil prices (   ) below $50 a barrel.(fall)

19. The players (   ) up at 6 o'clock.(get)

20. The policeman (   ) his lost wallet.(find)

8. 다음 문장의 (   ) 안에 과거동사를 쓰시오.

01. Two airplanes (   ) in the sky then.(fly)

02. The shop owner (   ) me not to go there.(tell)

03. The pitcher (   ) a ball to the batter.(throw)

04. They (   ) the children work for hours.(have)

05. I (   ) Jenny crying out in her room.(hear)

06. Mina (   ) a man baking delicious cakes.(see)

07. They (   ) people shouting in the cafe.(hear)

08. My wife (   ) very good about herself.(feel)

09. The man (   ) her a cup of coffee.(give)

〈정답과 해설 12P〉

10. The citizens (   ) his saying.(understand)

11. Boys (   ) their time on the game.(spend)

12. My grandfather (   ) upstairs after dinner.(go)

13. Those polar bears (   ) on melting ice.(stand)

14. My husband (   ) heavily last Friday night.(drink)

15. The woman (   ) something touching her back.(feel)

Chapter

05

Article
관사

부정관사 a(n)와 정관사 the

부정관사 a(n)	정관사 the
one이 약화된 표현으로 막연한 하나를 의미	this, that, these, those의 통합 형태

관사는 부정관사 a(n)와 정관사 the가 있다. 명사 앞에 사용하는 것으로 특별한 형용사의 일종으로 볼 수 있다.

Study 01 부정관사 a, an

부정관사 a(n)은 one이 약화된 표현으로 셀 수 있는 명사 중 구체적으로 정하지 않은 **막연한 하나**를 뜻하는 명사 앞에 붙인다. 셀 수 없는 명사에는 붙지 않는다.

a나 an은 뒤에 오는 명사의 발음에 따라 달라진다. 즉 발음이 모음발음 [æ,ʌ,ə,ɑ,ɛ,e,u 등]이면 an을 쓰고 자음발음이면 a를 쓴다.

1. an

⊙ [æ, ʌ, ə, ɑ,ɛ, e, u 등 모음발음] 명사 앞에서 쓴다.

an example, an idea, an apple, an uncle, an umbrella, an old man, an hour, an elementary school

- My son has **an** apple in the morning.   나의 아들은 아침에 사과를 하나 먹는다.
- I'm looking for **an** MP3 player.   나는 MP3 플레이어를 찾고 있는 중이다.

2. a

⊙ [p, k, p, t,s, Θ, ʃ, tʃ, b, g, v, d, ʒ, dʒ, ð, r, j, h, w 등 자음발음] 앞에서 사용한다.

a door, a phone, a clock, a school, a story, a picture, a tree, a son, a year, a daughter, a host, a month, a doll, a tree, a comb, a computer, a university, a useful tool, a uniform, a wonderful time

• My daughter had **a** sweet potato last night. 나의 딸은 지난 밤 고구마를 하나 먹었다.

주의

① 철자가 u로 시작하는 단어는 발음에 따라 달라진다. 발음이 모음 [ʌ]로 시작하는 단어는 an을 붙인다. 하지만 발음이 자음 [j]로 시작하는 단어는 a를 붙인다.

[ʌ]로 시작하는 단어 – an uncle[ʌŋkl], an umbrella[ʌmbrélə],
[j]로 시작하는 단어 – a uniform[júːnəfɔ̀ːrm], a university[jùːnəvə̀ːrsəti], a useful app [júːsfəl æp], a unique style [juːníːk stail]

② h로 시작하는 단어는 첫 발음이 자음 [h]로 시작하는 단어는 a를 붙이고, 첫발음 h가 소리가 안 나는 묵음이어서 모음이 첫 발음인 경우는 an을 쓴다.

a hotdog[hɑ̀tdɔ́ːg], a house[haus], a high mountain[hai máuntən]
an hour[auər], an honest boy[ɑ̀nist bɔi]

🔍 확인문제 1

아래 명사 중에서 a나 an중 하나를 쓰시오.

(01). ___ minute   (02). ___ essential subject   (03). ___ fish

(04). ___ year   (05). ___ team   (06). ___ elephant

(07). ___ cartoon   (08). ___ bookcase   (09). ___ trash can

(10). ___ elevator   (11). ___ cabinet   (12). ___ uncle

(13). ___ calender   (14). ___ refrigerator   (15). ___ apple

〈정답과 해설 12P〉

Study 02 정관사 the

정해 졌다는 뜻의 정관사 the는 정한다는 개념이 있을 때 모두 쓸 수 있다. 즉 **앞에 나온 명사**라든가, the sun 등 **하나 밖에 없는 것**, Open the window 같은 대화당사자들 끼리 마음속으로 **뻔히 아는 것**, 그 말자체가 정해지는 의미가 있는 순서를 나타내는 the first ~ , the second ~ 등 서수, '가장 ~한'의 뜻의 **최상급**, **the only 명사, the same 명사, the very 명사, the last 명사** 등에서 처럼 **정하는 의미가 있는 어구**에 the를 붙인다.

---

① 앞에 나온 명사를 다시 쓸 때

- Mom bought **a car**, and **the car** is very expensive. 나는 차를 한 대 샀다. 그런데 그 차는 매우 비싸다.

② 대화 당사자 간 뻔히 아는 것

- What's **the matter**? 무엇이 문제인가?
- We can find it on **the Internet**. 우리는 인터넷에서 그것을 찾을 수 있다.

③ 세상에 하나밖에 없어서 명백한 것

- **The moon** shines on the village. 달이 그 마을에 비춘다.
- They trip **the world** together. 그들은 함께 전 세계 여행 했다.

④ 순서를 나타내는 서수

- Our team got **the first prize** in the contest. 우리 팀은 콘테스트에서 우승했다.

⑤ 최상급

- This road is **the best way** we can go to New York. 이 길은 우리가 뉴욕에 갈 수 있는 최고의 길이다.
- This is **the highest** building in the world. 이것은 세계에서 가장 높은 빌딩이다.

⑥ 지정하는 의미가 있는 말들

  the only 명사, the very 명사, the same 명사, the next 명사, the last 명사

- This is **the very seat** that I took yesterday in this theater. 이것은 내가 어제 극장에서 앉은 바로 그 의자이다.

⑦ 한정하는 말이 있을 때
- **The water** <u>in this well</u> is clean.　　　　　　　　　이 샘물은 깨끗하다.
- These are **the books** <u>that my son read</u> in his early days. 이것은 나의 아들이 어린 시절에 읽었던 책 들이다.

⑧ 악기 이름이 '연주하다(play)'와 함께 쓰일 때.
- Mike played **the cello** on the contest.　　　　　　마이크는 콘테스트에서 첼로를 연주했다.

　다만 play가 아닌 말과 쓰일 때는 the를 붙이지 않는다.
- I have a guitar.　　　　　　　　　　　　　　　　나는 기타를 가지고 있다.

⑨ 특정한 강, 바다 이름 등 고유명사
- **The Han river** is very wonderful at night.　　　　한강은 밤에 매우 멋지다.

정관사의 유래
정관사 the는 this나 that, these나 those의 통합형이다.

```
- this  셀 수 있는 단수명사
        셀 수 없는 단수명사        ⇒        the 단수명사
- that  셀 수 있는 단수명사
        셀 수 없는 단수명사
```

```
- these  셀 수 있는 복수명사      ⇒        the 복수명사
- those  셀 수 있는 복수명사
```

① the 셀 수 있는 단수명사 / 셀 수 없는 단수명사
　this나 that의 통합형으로 정하는 개념이 있는 셀 수 있는 단수명사에 the를 붙인다.
- this taxi(이 택시)와 that taxi(저 택시) ⇒ the taxi

　또 셀 수 없는 명사에서도 정하는 개념이 있을 때는 the를 붙일 수 있다.
- this water와 that water ⇒ the water

② the 셀 수 있는 복수명사
　복수명사에 붙은 these나 those의 통합형이다.
- these taxis(이 택시들)과 those taxis(저 택시들) ⇒ the taxis

아래 명사 앞 (　　　) 안에 정관사 the를 붙일 수 있는 것과 관사를 쓰지 않는 것으로 구별하시오.

(01). Please, close (　　　) book.

(02). (　　　) S(s)un shines in the sky.

(03). Please, turn on (　　　) light.

(04). (　　　) S(s)chool begins at 9 o'clock.

(05). The murderer went to (　　　) prison.

(06). The workers are paid by (　　　) day.

(07). Step down at (　　　) third station.

(08). Busan is (　　　) second city in Korea.

(09). They were having (　　　) breakfast then.

(10). (　　　) F(f)ather is at home, but mother is out.

(11). My son plays (　　　) piano well.

(12). (　　　) W(w)ater in this lake is clean.

(13). (　　　) B(b)ag on the desk is yours.

(14). Please, close (　　　) door. It is cold.

(15). The boys were playing (　　　) basketball.

〈정답과 해설 12P〉

🔍 확인문제 3

다음 문장들의 명사 앞 (   ) 안에 정관사 the를 붙이는 것은 O, 정관사 the를 붙이지 않는 것은 X 하시오.

(01). Sujin is (   ) only friend that I have.

(02). Sunday is (   ) first day of a week.

(03). (   ) H(h)ouse on the corner is for sale.

(04). My brother majors in (   ) politics.

(05). The boys have (   ) wisdom of Solomon.

(06). That man is (   ) principal of our school.

(07). Ted is (   ) only man suitable for the job.

(08). You must not make (   ) same mistakes.

(09). Seoul is (   ) largest city in South Korea.

(10). This is (   ) book that I borrowed from him.

(11). He has a daughter and (   ) daughter is a doctor.

(12). The students go to school by (   ) train every morning.

(13). I met a girl, and (   ) girl showed me the way to the post office.

(14). The farmer found a bag in the field, and the bag is full of (   ) gold.

(15). The reservoir in the town is full of (   ) water in spring.

〈정답과 해설 12~13P〉

Study 03 부정관사 a(n)도, 복수형 –(e)s도 붙이지 않는 명사

셀 수 있는 명사중 ~(e)s를 붙이지 않는 복수형 명사	셀 수 없는 명사

1. 셀 수 있는 명사 중 –(e)s 붙이지 않고 복수형 만드는 명사

–(e)s 붙이지 않는 복수형 명사: 셀 수 있는 명사이지만, 복수형 만들 때 –(e)s를 붙이지 않는 특별한 셀 수 있는 명사이다. 이 복수형 명사는 막연한 하나가 아니므로 부정관사 a(n)도 붙이지 않는다.

people, deer, sheep, fish, teeth, men, women, mice, feet, geese, children 등

셀 수 있는 명사는 보통 정하는 개념이 없는 막연한 하나일 때 a나 an을 붙이고, 둘 이상은 명사에 –(e)s를 붙인다.

- a tip – tips
- a hobby – hobbies
- a teethbrush – toothbrushes
- a phone – phones
- a box – boxes
- a book – books

- a way – ways
- a field – fields

- a clock – clocks
- a leaf – leaves
- a calender – calenders

- a job-jobs

2. 셀 수 없는 명사

셀 수 없는 명사는 두 개가 될 수 없으므로 두 개 이상 중에서 막연한 하나를 말하는 부정관사 a(n)을 붙이지도 않고 복수형 –(e)s도 붙이지 않는다.

① 고유명사

   a(n)은 여러 개 중에서 정하지 않은 막연한 하나를 가리킬 때 사용하므로, 하나밖에 없는 고유명사인 사람이름이나 지역명 등은 관사를 일반적으로 붙이지 않는다.

   Ahn Joong-Geun, Kim Gu, Socrates, Seoul, Asia, Africa 등의 고유명사에는 부정관사 a(n)을 붙이지 않는다.

② 물질명사

   stone(석재), wood(목재), water, coffee, gas 와 같은 고체나 액체, 기체를 말하는 물질명사도 셀 수 없는 명사 이므로 a(n)을 붙이지 않는다.

③ 셀 수 없는 추상명사

   눈이 보이지 않는 어떤 개념을 말하는 추상적인 명사도 a(n)을 쓰지 않는다 .

   • truth(진실), history(역사), science(과학), mathematics(수학) 등

다만 셀 수 없는 명사라고 하더라도 정해진 개념이 있을 때는 정관사 the를 붙일 수 있다.
• **The gold** <u>in this ring</u> is 18k.   이 반지의 금은 18k이다.

확인문제 4

다음 명사에서 a(n)을 쓸 수 있는 것은 O, 쓸 수 없는 것은 × 하시오. 또 셀 수 있는 명사와 셀 수 없는 명사 두 가지 모두로 쓰일 수 있는 것도 찾으시오.

(01). breakfast   (02). banana   (03). sugar

(04). flour   (05). snow   (06). rice

(07). Mike   (08). Mt. Everst   (09). pleasure

(10). cup

〈정답과 해설 13P〉

확인문제 5

다음 명사 앞에 부정관사 a나 an, 관사 쓰지 않는 무 관사(×) 중 하나를 쓰시오.

(01). ___ picture   (02). ___ desk   (03). ___ gas

(04). ___ umbrella   (05). ___ house   (06). ___ honor

(07). ___ chair   (08). ___ board   (09). ___ computer

(10). ___ woman   (11). ___ mountain   (12). ___ store

(13). ___ bread   (14). ___ bag   (15). ___ clock

(16). ___ air conditioner (17). ___ heater   (18). ___ cook

(19). ___ smart phone (20). ___ sugar

〈정답과 해설 13P〉

확인문제 6

다음 명사 앞에 부정관사 a나 an, 정관사 the, 그리고 관사 쓰지 않는 무 관사(×) 중 하나를 쓰시오.

(01). ___ ball pen   (02). ___ speaker   (03). ___ armchair

(04). ___ sun   (05). ___ salt water (06). ___ table

(07). ___ star   (08). ___ engineer   (09). ___ egg

(10). ___ farmer   (11). ___ uniform   (12). ___ university

(13). ___ English teacher (14). ___ useful tip (15). ___ food

(16). ___ honest man   (17). ___ hour   (18). ___ European

(19). ___ bottle   (20). ___ world

〈정답과 해설 13P〉

further study 명사와 관사

명사 셀 수 있는 명사와 셀 수 없는 명사

셀 수 있는 명사		셀 수 없는 명사	
하나 일 때, 부정관사 a(n), 둘 이상일 때, –(e)s 와 함께 쓸 수 있다. – 일반 보통명사 – 구체적 행위나 상황 추상명사 – 덩어리를 말하는 집합명사		a나 an과 함께 쓰일 수 없고, 복수형을 만들기 위하여 –(e)s와도 쓸 수 없다. 당연히 단수명사로 만 사용한다. – 물질명사(고체, 액체, 기체) – 개념을 표현하는 셀 수 없는 추상명사 (학문, 스포츠, 계절, 식사, 병 등 명칭) – 일반적인 고유명사	※ a(n) 도 –(e)s 도 붙이지 않는 명사
단수명사	복수명사		
a(n) 단수명사	명사(e)s		
	–(e)s 없는 복수명사		
the 단수/복수명사		the 단수명사	

명사는 '**셀 수 있는 명사**'와 '**셀 수 없는 명사**'가 있다. **셀 수 있는 명사**는 '정하지 않는 막연한 하나'를 말할 때 a(n)을 쓰며, 두 개 이상일 때는 명사 끝에 –(e)s를 쓴다. 다만 people, fish, deer 등 '–(e)s'를 쓰지 않고 복수형을 만드는 **셀 수 있는 명사**도 있다.

하지만 셀 수 없는 명사는 정하지 않는 막연한 하나나 둘 이상이 될 수 없으므로 부정관사 a(n)도 복수형 –(e)s를 쓸 수 없다.

A. 셀 수 있는 명사

막연한 하나 일 때, a(n)을 붙일 수 있다.

단수명사	복수명사
'a(n) 단수명사'	'명사-(e)s'
	-(e)s 안 붙이는 복수명사

일반적으로 셀 수 있는 명사는 막연한 하나일 때, 구체적으로 정해지지 않았다는 뜻인 부정관사 a(n)을 쓰거나 둘 이상일 때는 -(e)s를 쓴다. 다만 people, men, teeth 등 -(e)s를 쓰지 않는 복수 명사도 있다.

① 보통명사 - 일반적으로 단수는 a(n)을 사용하고 복수는 -(e)s를 쓴다.
  • a book-books, a boy-boys, a desk-desks, a phone-phones, a room- rooms, a prison - prisons

② 셀 수 있는 추상명사 - 형태가 없는 추상명사이지만 구체적 행위나 상황을 나타내는 말로 셀 수 있다. 보통명사처럼 보통 단수는 a(n)을 사용하고 복수는 -(e)s를 쓸 수 있다.
  • a minute - minutes, an hour - hours, a day - days, a night - nights, a year - years,
    a worry - worries, a dream - dreams

③ 집합덩어리와 구성원들 두 가지로 사용되는 것: 집합덩어리는 단수, 구성원을 가리킬 때는 복수취급 한다. 또 집합덩어리가 하나일 때는 단수, 여러 개 일 때는 복수로 쓴다.
  • family(가족-단수/ 가족구성원들-복수): a family 한 가족, families (여러)가족 들

  • class(학급-단수/ 학생들-복수): a class 한 학급, classes(여러)학급 들

다만, 셀 수 있는 명사라고 하더라도 -(e)s를 쓰지 않는 복수명사들도 있다.
  • a man-men, a woman-women, a tooth-teeth, a child-children, a fish-fish, a deer-deer, a
    sheep-sheep, people 사람들, cattle 소들, the police경찰관 들,

결론적으로 셀 수 있는 명사는 -(e)s를 쓰지 않고 복수로 쓰이는 people, fish, deer, men, teeth 등의 명사를 제외하고는 a(n)을 붙여서 막연한 하나를 칭하거나 -(e)s를 붙여 복수형을 만든다.

B. 셀 수 없는 명사

막연한 하나를 말하는 부정관사 a(n)을 붙이지 않는다.

일반적인 물질명사	개념을 표현하는 추상명사	고유명사

셀 수 없는 명사는 정하지 않은 하나를 뜻 하는 부정관사 a(n)을 붙이지도 않고 복수형을 만들기 위하여 –(e)s를 붙이지도 않는다.

① 물질명사(고체, 액체, 기체)
- 고체 – silver, bread, soap, waste, iron, wood, gold, stone
- 액체 – water, coffee, shampoo, wine
- 기체 – vapor, steam, air, gas

※ 온갖 잡탕명사

특히 아래 단어처럼 여러 가지 잡탕으로 이루어진 명사는 셀 수 없는 명사이다.
- clothing(pants, trousers, gloves, a necktie 등으로 구성)의류
- furniture(a chair, a desk, a table 등으로 구성)가구
- stationery(paper, a note, an eraser 등으로 구성)문구류
- equipment(스키장비, 골프장비 등으로 구성)장비
- machinery(a bus, a heater, a computer, a bike 등으로 구성)기계류
- baggage수화물

② 생각만 할 수 있는 개념을 말하는 셀 수 없는 추상명사

대표적인 셀 수 없는 추상명사에는 학문명, 식사명, 스포츠명, 계절명, 관직이나 신분 등이 있다.

– 학문명 – math, science, music, art, politics etc
- Do you want to major in <u>science</u>?　　　　　너는 과학을 전공하기를 원하니?

– 식사명 – breakfast, lunch, dinner, supper etc
- The soldiers had <u>lunch</u> at 2 o'clock.　　　　그 군인들은 두시에 점심을 먹었다.

– 스포츠명 – baseball, soccer, golf etc
- Emily often plays <u>tennis</u> on Sundays.　　　Emily는 가끔 일요일에 테니스를 친다.

– 계절명 – spring, summer, fall, winter etc
- My young brother was born in <u>summer</u>.　　나의 동생은 여름에 태어났다.

- 추상적인 개념- church 예배, school 학습, bed 수면(잠), prison 구속
- The students in the middle school go to <u>school</u> at 9 o'clock.

중학교 학생들은 9시에 학교에 간다.(공부하러 간다)

- 개념에 해당하는 교통통신- bus, taxi, train, telephone, airplane etc
- They went to Seoul by <u>bus</u>.   그들은 버스(라는 교통방식)로 서울에 간다.
- We send a message by <u>email</u>.   우리는 이메일(이라는 방식)으로 메시지를 보낸다.

-가족 구성원- mom, dad, mother, father 등
- <u>Mom</u> called me in London in the morning.   엄마는 런던에서 아침에 전화했다.

- 관직이나 신분
- <u>Mayor</u> Park visited the orphanage.   박시장은 고아원을 방문했다.

- 일반적인 개념
- advice 충고, information 정보, hope 희망, peace 평화, belief 믿음, money 돈, freedom 자유, life 삶, love 사랑, truth 진실, kindness 친절, beauty 아름다움, friendship 우정 etc

주의   -s가 붙어있으나 원래 단어가 그렇게 생겼을 뿐 복수가 아닌 것

news 뉴스, means 수단, measles 홍역, economics 경제학, physics 물리학

③ 고유명사
- Yi Sun-sin, Seoul, Asia, Africa, China, Russia

C. 구체적으로 정하는 정관사 the

'셀 수 있는 명사'(단수이든 복수이든)와 '셀 수 없는 명사' 모두, 정하는 의미가 있을 때에는 the는 모두 붙일 수 있다.

셀 수 있는 명사		the 셀 수 없는 명사(단수)
the 단수형명사	the 복수형명사	**the water** <u>in the lake</u>
the boy	the boys	

Level UP

뜻에 따라 셀 수 있는 명사가 되기도 하고 셀 수 없는 명사가 되기도 하는 것

몇몇 명사는 뜻에 따라 셀 수 있는 명사가 되기도 하고 셀 수 없는 명사가 되기도 한다.
셀 수 있는 명사에는 a(n)을 붙여서 단수형을 만들거나, –(e)s를 붙여 복수형을 만들기도 한다.
셀 수 없는 명사에는 a(n)이나 –(e)s를 붙이지 않는다.

명사	셀 수 있는 명사	셀 수 없는 명사
school	학교(a school/schools)	수업
prison	교도소(a prison/prisons)	수감
church	교회(a church/churches)	예배
bed	침대(a bed/beds)	잠
stone	돌멩이(a stone/stones)	석재
bus	버스(a bus/buses)	버스라는 교통방식
train	열차(a train/trains)	열차라는 교통방식

셀 수 있는 명사로 사용된 경우
• There are <u>three schools</u> in this town.　이 읍내에 3개의 학교가 있다.

셀 수 없는 명사로 사용된 경우
• The students go to <u>school</u> at 9 o'clock.　학생들은 아홉시에 학교에 간다.

아래 굵은 글씨체의 명사가 셀 수 있는 명사로 사용 되었는지 셀 수 없는 명사로 사용되었는지를 쓰고 그 명사의 뜻을 쓰시오. 그리고 문장을 해석하시오.

(01). How many **churches** are in Korea?

(/   /   )

(02). Why do you go to **church**?

(/   /   )

(03). I bought **a bed** last weekend.

(/   /   )

(04). My daughter goes to **bed** at 10.

(/   /   )

(05). The child threw **a stone** at the dog.

(/   /   )

(06). This bridge is made from **stone**.

(/   /   )

(07). The passengers changed **buses** at London.

(/   /   )

(08). The passengers went to the park by **bus**.

(/   /   )

(09). There are 12 **trains** for Mokpo a day.

(/   /   )

(10). We want to go to Paris by **train**.

(/   /   )

〈정답과 해설 13P〉

Grammar in Reading

〈정답과 해설 13~14P〉

1. 다음 글에서 ( ) 안에 a(n), the 중 하나를 쓰거나 관사가 사용되지 않는 곳에는 ×를 쓰시오.

I am ⓐ ( ) man, but I can't move or speak. I have no legs but I can stand. I don't like ⓑ ( ) sun. I usually wear ⓒ ( ) white clothes. When it snows, children enjoy making me.

01. ⓐ-
02. ⓑ-
03. ⓒ-

2. 다음 대화를 읽고 ( ) 안에 a(n), the 중 하나를 쓰거나 관사가 사용되지 않는 곳에는 ×를 쓰시오.

Tony: You know what? ⓐ ( ) starfish has ⓑ ( ) eye at ⓒ ( ) end of each arm.
Alice: Really? If a starfish has 5 arms, does it have 5 eyes?
Tony: Sure, I read it on ⓓ ( ) Internet.
Alice: That's interesting.

01. ⓐ-
02. ⓑ-
03. ⓒ-
04. ⓓ-

3. 다음 대화를 읽고 ( ) 안에 a(n), the 중 하나를 쓰거나 관사가 사용되지 않는 곳에는 ×를 쓰시오.

Hi, my name is Peter. I'd like to introduce my family. My father is ⓐ ( ) musician. He is very good at playing ⓑ ( ) piano. My mother is ⓒ ( ) teacher. She loves working with kids. My sister is a cook. She works at ⓓ ( ) restaurant. My brother is a doctor. He takes care of sick people.

01. ⓐ-
02. ⓑ-
03. ⓒ-
04. ⓓ-

Grammar in Reading

4. 다음 글에서 ( ) 안에 a(n), the 중 하나를 쓰거나 관사가 사용되지 않는 곳에는 ×를 쓰시오.

Sometimes scientists need to observe ⓐ ( ) object closely. Certain tools can help them observe details they might not be able to see using just their eyes.

ⓑ ( ) hand lens makes things look larger than they are. It magnifies them. Hold ⓒ ( ) lens a few centimeters in front of your eye. Then move ⓓ ( ) object closer to the lens until you can see it clearly. Never let the lens touch your eye. Never use it to look at ⓔ ( ) sun.

(지문 출처– 〈Science〉 from Harcourt School Publishers)

01. ⓐ–
02. ⓑ–
03. ⓒ–
04. ⓓ–
05. ⓔ–

5. 다음 글에서 ( ) 안에 a(n), the 중 하나를 쓰거나 관사가 사용되지 않는 곳에는 ×를 쓰시오.

I am ⓐ ( ) student. I go to ⓑ ( ) school everyday. Every morning my mother says to me, "Come back home early." Then I say to my mother, "Mom, I am not ⓒ ( ) baby. I am now ⓓ ( ) adult. Don't worry about me." My mother says, "You are not ⓔ ( ) adult. You are not mature enough. The night is dangerous for ⓕ ( ) young girl like you." My mother loves me, and she always worries about me. My mother is tall and thin, but I am not tall. My father is short. I think that I resemble my father. My father is not ⓖ ( ) child. He is ⓗ ( ) adult, but my mother always says to him, "Come back home early."

01. ⓐ–
02. ⓑ–
03. ⓒ–
04. ⓓ–
05. ⓔ–
06. ⓕ–
07. ⓖ–
08. ⓗ–

Grammar in Reading

〈정답과 해설 14P〉

6. 다음 글에서 ( ) 안에 a(n), the 중 하나를 쓰거나 관사가 사용되지 않는 곳에는 ×를 쓰시오.

I have ⓐ ( ) younger sister. She is four years old. She does not understand ⓑ ( ) sun and ⓒ ( ) moon. She asks me at ⓓ ( ) night, "Is that the sun?", and I answer, "No, it is not. It is the moon." She asks me by day, "Is that the moon?", and I answer, "No, it is not. It is the sun."

My sister likes to paint pictures, and she always asks me about the colors. "Is ⓔ ( ) sky blue?" she asks. "Yes, it is. It is blue," I answer. "Are those things in ⓕ ( ) sky clouds?" she asks. "Yes, they are. They are clouds," I answer. "Are those clouds black?" she asks. "No, they are not. They are white," I answer. My sister bothers me with many questions, but I love her.

01. ⓐ-
02. ⓑ-
03. ⓒ-
04. ⓓ-
05. ⓔ-
06. ⓕ-

7. 다음 글에서 ( ) 안에 a(n), the 중 하나를 쓰거나 관사가 사용되지 않는 곳에는 ×를 쓰시오.

I see ⓐ ( ) old man on my way to ⓑ ( ) school every morning. He sits on ⓒ ( ) bench at the bus stop and asks me ⓓ ( ) same questions everyday. "Hey, boy. Who are you?" he asks. "I am ⓔ ( ) student at Seoul Elementary School. My name is Tom," I answer. "What is that?" he asks. "It is our school bus," I answer. "Who are they in the school bus?" he asks. "They are my friends," I answer. "They look like my grandson. Who is ⓕ ( ) man next to your friends?" he asks. "He is my teacher. He teaches us ⓖ ( ) history," I answer. "He looks like my son. My son and my grandson live in Busan City. It is very far from here. I miss my family," he says. Many people think that the old man is insane, but I don't think so. He just feels lonely.

01. ⓐ-
02. ⓑ-
03. ⓒ-
04. ⓓ-
05. ⓔ-
06. ⓕ-
07. ⓖ-

〈정답과 해설 15P〉

1. 다음 명사에서 a(n)을 쓸 수 있는 것은 O, 쓸 수 없는 것은 × 하시오. 또 두 가지 모두로 쓰일 수 있는 것도 찾으시오.

01. tree (　　) 　　02. wood (　　) 　　03. train (　　)

04. bus (　　) 　　05. bench (　　) 　　06. money (　　)

07. beer (　　) 　　08. yellow (　　) 　　09. girl (　　)

10. happiness (　　) 　　11. peace (　　) 　　12. stone (　　)

13. water (　　) 　　14. coffee (　　) 　　15. gas (　　)

16. earth (　　) 　　17. truck (　　) 　　18. spoon (　　)

19. freedom (　　) 　　20. violin (　　) 　　21. piano (　　)

22. book (　　) 　　23. cake (　　) 　　24. advice (　　)

25. information (　　) 　　26. furniture (　　) 　　27. stationery (　　)

28. equipment (　　) 　　29. baggage (　　) 　　30. piece (　　)

2. 다음 문장에서 관사를 붙이지 않는 것을 찾아 ×하시오. 또 반드시 정관사 the를 붙여야 하는 것을 골라 the를 쓰시오.

01. (　　　) W(w)ater is essential to life

02. (　　　) S(s)un shines at the sea.

03. The bride bought (　　　) furniture.

04. (　　　) M(m)oon is bright here.

05. (　　　) B(b)ooks give man vigor.

06. They waited at (　　　) crossroad in the coner.

07. (　　　) C(c)lothing in the store is cheap.

08. We used to play in (　　　) Han river when we were young.

09. The player is (　　　) first baseman.

10. I bought a book and read (　　　) book.

11. Bring me (　　　) books on the desk.

12. My wife likes (　　　) car that I bought.

13. This is (　　　) car which I rented yesterday.

14. She plays (　　　) violin everyday.

15. They play (　　　) soccer on Sundays.

3. 다음 문장에서 관사를 붙이지 않는 것을 찾아 ×하시오. 또 반드시 정관사 the를 붙여야 하는 것을 골라 the를 쓰시오.

01. (　　　) M(m)an on the stage is the famous pianist.

02. (　　　) B(b)ean in the basket was harvested this fall.

03. My birthday is (　　　) fourth day of September.

04. This is (　　　) only man I know in this village.

05. He is (　　　) same man that played the main role in the movie.

06. We missed (　　　) last train for Suwon.

07. My daughter has (　　　) breakfast at Seven.

〈정답과 해설 15P〉

08. Becky is (   ) most handsome student in our class.

09. The children go to (   ) school at 8 o'clock.

10. The Chinese don't go to (   ) church on Sundays.

11. They used to meet at the park after (   ) dinner.

12. The soldiers go to (   ) bed at 10 o'clock.

13. How about having (   ) lunch together?

14. Please, close (   ) door.

15. That man is (   ) very man that stole the bag.

Chapter

06

Preposition
전치사

전치사는 명사가 놓여있는 위치와 장소의 상태를 표현하다. 시간에도 그 위치와 장소의 상태의 원리가 그대로 표현한다.

Study 01 at, on, in

at은 공간에서 '~지점'을 표현한다. on은 접촉을 나타낸다. 접촉의 의미는 추상적으로 '관련'을 나타낼 수 있다. 시간적으로 접촉된 '~하자마자'를 나타내기도 한다. in은 '~안'을 표현한다. 추상적으로 '~분야에서'를 나타낼 수 있다.

시간에서 at은 시각, 밤, 정오 등을 나타내고 on은 날짜, 요일, in은 계절, 년도, 월, 아침, 점심, 정오 일 때 쓴다. (at시밤정, on날요, in계년월아점저로 암기)

1. at : ~점에

① 좁은 장소
 • KTX of Honam Line stops at Iksan station.

호남선 KTX는 익산역에서 정차한다.

▶ KTX 호남선

- My mother is **at** a clothes shop.
- Luisa hesitated **at** the park entrance.
- Susan is studying Korean **at** university.

② 시간, 밤(night), 정오(noon)앞에서 <at 시/밤/정>
- My father goes to work **at** 8:00.
- My sister and I go to school **at** 9:00.
- Boys used to watch stars **at** night.

나의 엄마는 옷가게에 있다.
루이사는 공원입구에서 주저했다.
수잔은 대학에서 한국어를 공부하고 있는 중이다. .

나의 아버지는 8시에 일하러 간다.
나의 누이와 나는 아홉시에 학교에 간다.
소년들은 밤에 별들을 보곤 했다.

2. on : 접촉

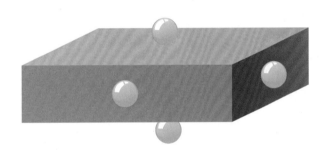

① 접촉(~위, 아래, 옆 등)
- The artist's work hangs **on** the wall.
- I like to lie **on** my bedroom.
- An old man sits **on** the bench at the bus stop.
- The cat jumped **on** the bed.
- Two little monkeys jumped **on** the bed.

그 예술가의 작품이 벽에 걸려 있다.
나는 나의 침실에서 누워 있기를 좋아한다.
노인은 버스 정류장 벤치에 앉아 있다.
고양이가 침대위로 점프했다.
두마리의 어린 원숭이가 침대에 점프했다.

② ~하자마자(시간적으로 연결)
- **On** seeing the policeman, he ran away.

경찰관을 보자마자 도망갔다.

③ 날짜, 요일 앞에서 <on 날/요>
- I'm usually at home **on** Sunday.
- **On** March 3, 1887, Annie moved to Alabama.

나는 보통 일요일에 집에 있다.
1887년 3월 3일에 Annie는 알라바마로 이사했다.

3. in : ～안에

① ～ 안에서

- A fly hid in the garbage can.   파리가 쓰레기통 안에서 숨었다.
- It's one of famous stories in the world.   그것은 세계에서 유명한 이야기들 중 하나이다.
- I met your sister in the shopping mall.   나는 쇼핑몰 안에서 너의 누이를 만났다.

② 계절, 년도, 월, 아침(in the morning), 점심(in the afternoon), 저녁(in the evening)

    \<in 계/년/월/아/점/저\>

- It rains a lot in summer.   여름에 비가 많이 내린다.
- She was born in 1979.   그녀는 1979년에 태어났다.
- There is much snow in December.   12월에 많은 눈이 온다.
- The farmers work hard in the morning.   농부들은 아침에 열심히 일한다.

③ 분야

- Are you interested in photography?   사진 찍기에 관심이 있나요?

확인문제 1

다음 빈칸에 at, on, in 중에서 알맞은 전치사를 골라 쓰시오.

(01). _____ winter

(02). _____ April

(03). _____ 10:20 p.m.

(04). _____ night

(05). _____ summer

(06). _____ Monday

(07). _____ April. 16.

(08). _____ the morning

(09). _____ noon

(10). _____ 9 o'clock

〈정답과 해설 15P〉

확인문제 2

다음문장에서 빈칸에 at, on, in 중에서 알맞은 전치사를 넣으시오.

(01). My mom drops me off _____ school.

(02), The television is _____ the living room.

(03). There are three bedrooms _____ our apartment.

(04). His father will go abroad _____ June.

(05). The people turns _____ the air conditioner.

(06). Bora finds some information _____ the Internet.

(07). Many artists make beautiful creations _____ computers.

(08). I played computer games until two _____ the morning.

(09). Today I am planning to meet my friend online _____ 9 pm.

(10). You really shouldn't play computer games until late _____ night.

〈정답과 해설 15P〉

Study 02
over와 under / above와 below along과 across

over와 under
보통 공간적으로 쓰인다. over는 떨어진 위, under는 떨어진 아래를 나타낸다.

1. over : (공간을 두고) ~ 위

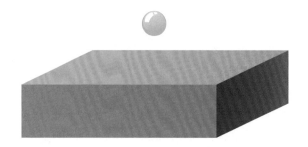

~ 위에

- A few butterflies are flying **over** the flowers.

  몇 마리의 잠자리가 꽃 위에서 날고 있는 중이다.

- Let's hang the painting **over** the fireplace.

  그 그림을 난로 위에 걸자. .

2. under : (공간을 두고) ~ 아래

~ 아래에

- There are some books under the table.
- My science notebook was under the desk.

테이블 아래에 얼마간의 책들이 있다.
제 과학 공책이 책상 아래에 있었다.

 beneath- under가 '(떨어진) 아래에'를 나타내지만 beneath는 '(접촉된) 아래에'에 많이 쓰인다.

The boat sank beneath the waves.
그 보트가 파도 속으로 잠겼다.

They found the body beneath a pile of leaves.
그들은 나뭇잎더미 아래에서 시체를 찾았다.

The submarine waited far beneath the ship.
잠수함이 배아래 멀리서 배를 기다렸다.

above

 below

3. above : (저멀리) 위

① ~ 위에

- Hover board floats above the ground. Hover 보드가 땅위에서 떠서 달린다.
- Raise your arms above your head. 너의 팔을 머리 위로 올려라.

② (지위나 신분이) ~ 위

- A general is above a mayor. 장군이 시장보다 위이다.

4. below : (저멀리) 아래

① ~ 아래에

- A skirt must be below the knee. 치마는 무릎 아래로 내려 와야 한다.

② (지위나 신분이) ~아래

- A captain is below a general. 선장은 장군 아래다.

5. along : ~ 를 따라서

- The boys walked <mark>along</mark> the street.
- An ivy plant spreads its stems <mark>along</mark> a brick wall.

그 소년들은 거리를 따라 걸었다.
담쟁이 넝쿨이 벽돌 벽을 따라 그것의 줄기를 퍼뜨린다.

6. across: ~ 를 가로 질러

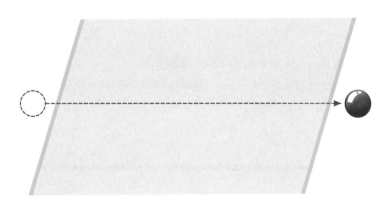

- Maddie ran <mark>across</mark> the yard.
- We watched the birds flying <mark>across</mark> the sky.
- Sometimes camels bring people <mark>across</mark> the desert.

Maddie는 뜰을 가로질러 달렸다.
우리는 새들이 하늘을 가로 질러 날고 있는 것을 보았다.
때때로 낙타는 사람들을 태우고 사막을 가로 지른다.

before 와 after

before는 공간적으로 '～ 앞에'를 나타내며 시간적으로 '～한 전에'를 나타낸다. 또한 after는 공간적으로 '～뒤에'를 나타내며 시간적으로 '～한 후에'를 표현한다. 추상적으로 '～를 추격하여'의 의미로 쓰이기도 한다.

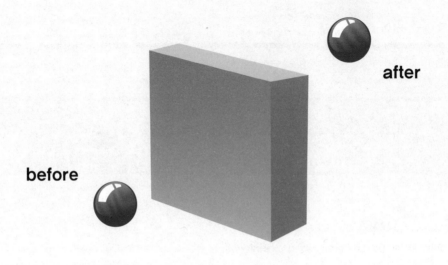

7. before : ～ 앞

⊙ ～ 앞에

• The bus stop is just before the school.

버스 정류장이 그 학교 바로 앞에 있다.

⊙ ～ 이전에

• The climbers arrived at the peak of the mountain before us.

그 등산객들은 우리보다 먼저 그 산 정상에 도착했다.

8. after : ～ 뒤

⊙ ～ 뒤에

• The detective runs after the criminal.

그 탐정은 그 범인을 추격한다.

⊙ ～ 한 후에

• After dinner the friend drank some whiskey and then drove home.

점심 후에 그 친구들은 얼마간의 위스키를 마시고 그런 다음 집으로 운전하여 갔다.

확인문제 3

아래 문장의 빈칸에 아래 보기에서 골라 적절한 전치사를 넣으시오.

over   under   before   after   along   across

(01). My cats run _____ the mice.

(02). The whales swim _____ the sea.

(03). A dragonfly is flying _____ your head.

(04). There are two cats _____ the table.

(05). The bicycles passed _____ the river bank

(06). We are going to play soccer _____ school.

《정답과 해설 16P》

Study 03 · from과 to / for와 during between과 among

> **from과 to**
> from은 '출발지점'을 나타내며 to는 도착지점을 표현한다.

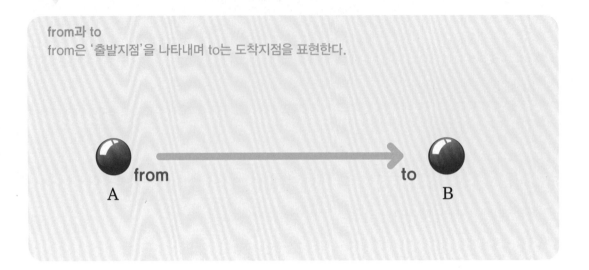

1. from : 출발지점

⊙ ~ 로부터(출발하여)

• My roommate is Paula from Peru.	나의 룸메이트는 페루출신의 Paula이다.
• More crocodiles rise from the wet swamp.	더 많은 악어들이 습지로부터 나온다.
• "We can do it" a voice from the swamp rumbles.	늪에서 "We can do it" 라는 목소리가 들렸다.
• A hot spring comes from heat within the ground.	온천은 땅 안에 있는 열로부터 나온다.

2. to : 도착지점

⊙ ~ 에(도착하여)

• We prefer going to an amusement park. 놀이공원 가는 게 더 좋아요.

• The pollen of these flowers is carried to other flowers by the wind.

이 꽃들의 화분은 바람에 의해 다른 꽃들로 옮겨진다.

CF from A to B: A에서 B까지

The festival will be held from 8th to 11th. 축제가 8일부터 11일까지 개최될 예정이다.

The cyclists takes four days to cycle from London to Edinburgh.

그 사이클리스트들은 런던에서 에딘버러까지 4일 걸린다.

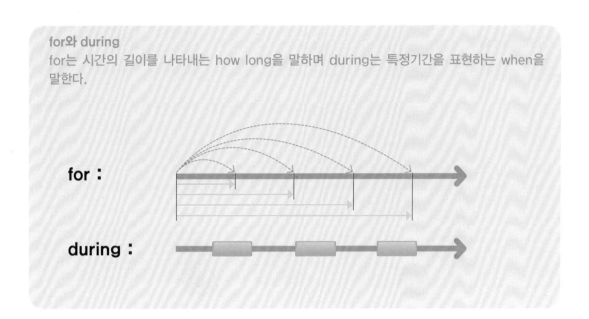

for와 during
for는 시간의 길이를 나타내는 how long을 말하며 during는 특정기간을 표현하는 when을 말한다.

for :

during :

3. for : 시간의 길이

- He hasn't eaten for ten days.   그는 10일 동안 먹지 않았다.
- I have been in Philadelphia for two weeks now.   나는 2주 동안 필라델피아에 있었다.

① 목적
- Scientists have created tissues for human organs.   과학자들은 인간의 장기를 위한 조직을 만들어 왔다.

② 원인
- Onyang is known for spring water.   온양은 그것의 온천물로 유명하다.

4. during : 특정시점

- Have you ever felt sick to your stomach during a test?
  너는 지금까지 시험동안에 너의 배가 아팠던 직이 있냐?
- The spring water is the bathing spot for royalty during the Joseon Danasty.
  온천물을 조선시대 동안에 왕족들을 위한 목욕탕이다

> **between과 among**
> between은 '둘 사이에'를 among는 '셋 이상 사이'를 나타낸다.

5. between : 둘 사이

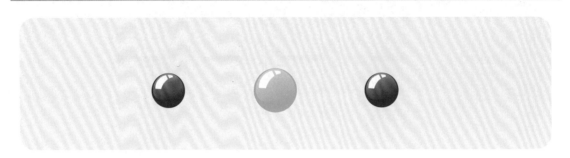

• The difference between social classes is huge.　　　사회계급들 간 차이는 거대하다.

• They called the time between two full moons a month.

　　　　　　그들은 두 개의 보름달 사이의 기간을 1개월 이라고 부른다.

6. among : 셋 이상 사이

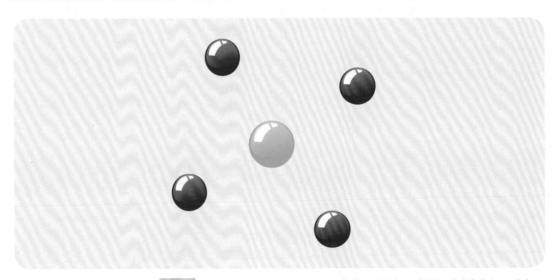

• The boys and girls play among pine trees.　　　소년과 소녀들은 소나무들 사이에서 놀고 있다.

🔍 확인문제 4

아래 문장의 빈칸에 아래 보기에서 골라 적절한 전치사를 넣으시오.

across	for	during	from	to	between	among

(01). _____ the day, they can see the sun.

(02). My family goes _____ the mountains in summer.

(03). I wandered around _____ hours with my only companion.

(04). _____ the night, they see the moon and many, many stars.

(05). All the food that our family eat comes _____ plants.

(06). We have a big opinion difference _____ my wife and me.

(07). Dung beetles are common _____ all continent.

(08). Peas, potatoes, carrots, cucumbers, and wheat all come _____ plants.

(09). People _____ different countries plays different sports.

(10). The pollen of these flowers is carried _____ other flowers by the wind.

《정답과 해설 16P》

Study 04 기타 다양한 전치사들

of와 with
of는 직접적, 간접적 관련, 혹은 부분을 나타낸다. with는 함께 공존하고 있는 주변의 상황을 나타낸다.

1. of : 부분, 직접 관련

① 적접적인 관련
- Motion is a sign of life.   동작은 삶의 신호이다.
- Beethoven's Sixth Symphony imitated the sound of a nightingale.
                                                                  베토벤 교향곡 6번은 나이팅게일의 소리를 모방한다.
- The mineral content in the water of many hot springs is high.
                                                                  많은 온천 물 속에 있는 미네랄 함유량이 높다.

② 부분
- Johnson was one of the best pitchers.   Johnson은 베스트 투수들 중 한명이다.

③ 재료
- The houses were made of wood.   그 집들은 나무로 만들어졌다.

2. with : 공존

① ~와 함께
- I eat an early dinner with my mom and my brother.
  나는 나의 엄마와 형과 함께 이른 저녁을 먹는다.

② 도구
- We can see cells with a microscope.
  우리는 현미경으로 세포를 볼 수 있다.

in front of 와 behind
in front of는 공간상에서 '∼ 앞에'를 나타내며 behind는 '∼ 뒤에서'를 나타낸다.

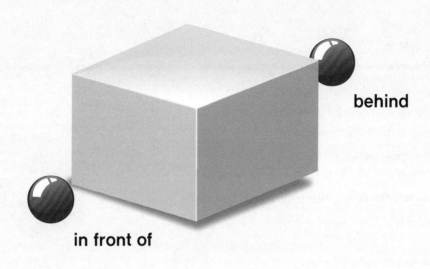

behind

in front of

3. in front of : ∼ 앞

⊙ ∼ 앞에

• The lion heard a baby crying in front of the door.　　그 사자가 아이가 문 앞에서 울고 있는 것을 들었다.

4. behind : ∼ 뒤

⊙ ∼ 뒤에

• The boy hid behind the building.　　그 소년은 건물 뒤에 숨었다.

> **by, about, near**
> by는 '~ 바로 옆에', about는 '~ 을 중심으로 여기저기, 즉 ~근처에', near는 '~ 가까이에'
> 를 표현한다.

5. by : 바로 옆

① ~ 옆에

- Jade was napping by the window.

  Jade는 창가에서 졸고 있는 중이었다.
- The dancers stood by the singer.

  댄서들은 그 가수 옆에 서있었다.
- The campers set up their tents by the sea shore.

  그 캠핑객들은 바닷가에 그들의 텐트를 쳤다.

② 수단

- The sailors travel by boat.

  그 선원들은 보트로 여행했다.

6. about : 주변

① ~ 주변에

- The travellers take a rest about the palace.

  그 여행객들은 궁궐 여기저기서 휴식을 취하고 있다.

② ~ 에 관하여

- Let's talk about our field trip.

  소풍에 대해 이야기해 봅시다.
- I'm thinking about joining the photo club this year.

  올해는 사진 동아리에 가입할까 생각 중이야.

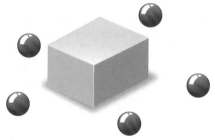

7. near : 가까이에

- Lionel lives near the river.

  Lionel은 강가에서 산다.

into와 out of
into는 '~ 안으로', out of는 '~ 밖으로'를 나타낸다.

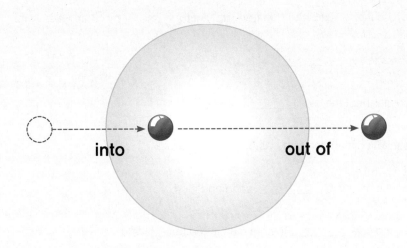

8. into : 안으로

① in(~ 안에서)과 to(~쪽으로)가 합해져서 '안쪽으로', 또는 추상적으로 '~으로 결과하여'의 뜻이다

• My cell phone fell into the toilet.	내 휴대 전화가 변기에 빠졌어.
• They heard someone coming into the room.	그들은 누군가 방안으로 들어오고 있는 것을 들었다.

② ~으로 결과하여

• Divide the square into right triangles.	사각형을 정삼각형으로 나누어라.
• 3D printers are turning dreams into reality.	3D 복사기들이 꿈을 현실화 하고 있는 중이다.

9. out of : 밖으로

• The robber ran out of the store.	그 강도는 가게 밖으로 달려 나왔다.
• The president got out of prison.	그 대통령은 감옥에서 석방되었다.

아래 문장의 빈칸에 아래 보기에서 골라 적절한 전치사를 넣으시오.

from	out of	behind	in front of	into	of	by	about	with

(01). His works tell us _____ his life.

(02). The soldier beat the dirt _____ these rugs.

(03). The sanitation man dumped waste _____ truck.

(04). The bricks are made _____ sand and mud.

(05). The young sat _____ the old man in the bus. (~ 옆에)

(06). Her friends put her ring _____ the clock. (~ 뒤에)

(07). We watched the cat nap _____ the fireplace.(~ 앞에)

(08). Eighteen percent _____ the lawmakers are nonwhite.

(09). A warm smile _____ twinkle eyes shows your happiness

(10). I moved my computer _____ my bedroom into the living room.

〈정답과 해설 16P〉

> **since와 through**
> since는 시간적으로 '〜 한 이후로(현재까지)', through는 공간상에서 '〜를 관통하여'의
> 의미로 쓰인다.

10. since : (과거 어느시점) 이후로

⊙ 과거의 어느 시점 이후로 현재까지로 쓰인다. 보통 현재까지를 나타낼 경우 'have/has + p.p'와 함께 많이 쓰인다.
   • String puppets have been used since the Middle Ages. 줄 인형은 중세 시대부터 쓰였다.

11. through : 통과

⊙ 〜 를 통과하여
   • Human waste is discharged through the anus.   인간의 배설물은 항문을 통해 버려진다.
   • We marched through the empty corridor.   우리는 텅 빈 복도를 가로 질러 행진했다.

within과 beyond
within은 '～ 이내에 있음'을 표현하며 beyond는 '～의 범위를 벗어나는'의 뜻으로 쓰인다.

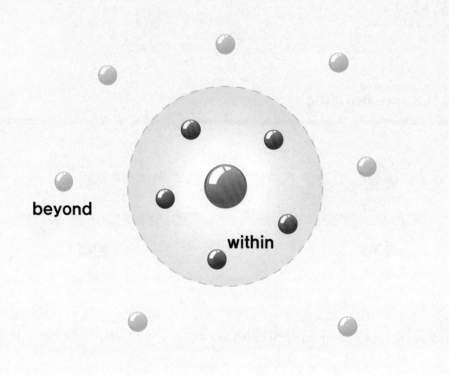

beyond

within

12. within : (영향력) 안에

⊙ '～ 안에 함께 있음'을 나타낸다. with(～ 함께)와 in (～ 안에)이 합해진 내용.

•We live and work within a browser.　　　　　　　우리는 브라우저 안에서 살고 일한다.

13. beyond : (영향력) 밖에

⊙ (～의 범위)를 넘어서

•The road continues beyond the villages up into the mountain.

　　　　　　　길은 마을을 넘어 올라가 산으로 계속 연결된다.

by와 until

by와 until 모두 우리말로 '~ 까지' 라는 뜻이다. 하지만 by는 '상황의 종료시점'을 표현하며
until은 '어떤 상황의 계속'을 말한다.

14. by : ~할 때까지 (완료시점)

• Can you finish the work by 9 o'clock?　　　　　너는 그 일을 9시까지 끝낼 수 있어요?

15. until : ~할 때 까지 (상황의 계속)

• Kids need help brushing until around age 8.

어린이는 약 8세 쯤 될 때까지 칫솔질하는 데 도움이 필요하다.

around(=round) ～ 둘레에

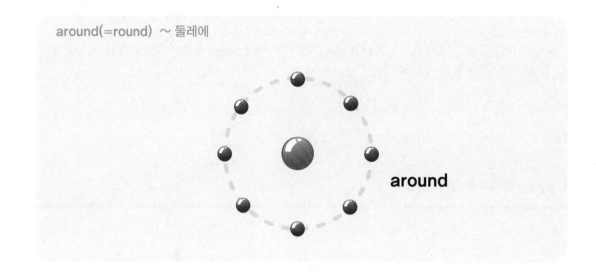

16. around (= round) : ～ 둘레에

• The moon moves around the earth.   달은 지구주위를 돈다.
• Bora looks around her desk.   보라는 책상 주변을 둘러보았다.
• The policeman walked around the car.   그 경찰관은 그 차 주변을 돌아봤다.

🔍 확인문제 6

아래 문장의 빈칸에 아래 보기에서 골라 적절한 전치사를 넣으시오.

| through | within | around | since | beyond | by | until |

(01). The boat sailed its way _____ the fog.

(02). The earth goes _____ the sun.

(03). The light comes _____ a window.

(04). We are now _____ sight of the island.(안에)

(05). We need to buy the book _____ next month.(～까지)

(06). She continued his working _____ her death.

(07). The war situation is _____ our control.(넘어선)

(08). They have stayed in London _____ last month.(~한 이후로)

(09). The soldiers are _____ range of enemy fire.(안에)

(10). Bob has been in the hospital _____ the car accident.(~한 이후로)

〈정답과 해설 16P〉

보통 추상적으로 쓰는 전치사
as – ~로서, like- ~처럼, without-~ 없이, against- ~ 에 저항하여

17. as : ~로서

• Using gardening as a health care tool is blossoming.   건강관리도구로서 정원손질을 이용하는 것은 축복이다.

18. like : ~처럼

• He cried like a baby.   그는 어린 아이처럼 울었다.
• He seems like an idiot.   그는 바보처럼 보인다.

19. without : ~없이

• We can't enter the foreign countries without a passport.

우리는 여권 없이 외국에 입국할 수 없다.

20. against : ~에 기대어

① ~에 기대어

- The man left his bicycle **against** fence.
- The snow is beating heavily **against** my tower.

그 남자는 그의 자전거를 펜스에 기대어 놓았다.

눈이 나의 타워에 세차게 때리고 있다.

② 대항하여

- We must fight **against** injustice.

우리는 불의와 싸워야 한다.

🔍 확인문제 7

아래 문장의 빈칸에 아래 보기에서 골라 적절한 전치사를 넣으시오.

like	as	without	against

(01). People view it _____ evolution.

(02). A bagel looks _____ a doughnut.

(03). _____ water, we are unable to survive.

(04). He guarded the building _____ thieves.

(05). His talent _____ a film director were soon regarded.

(06). My younger brother wants to be a famous singer _____ Psy.

〈정답과 해설 16P〉

Level UP 명사의 자리를 만들어 주는 전치사

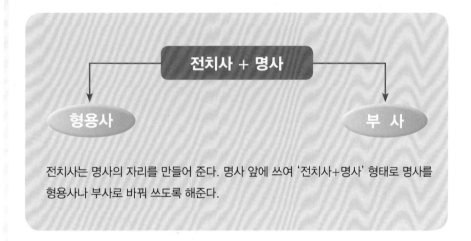

전치사는 명사의 자리를 만들어 준다. 명사 앞에 쓰여 '전치사+명사' 형태로 명사를 형용사나 부사로 바꿔 쓰도록 해준다.

A. 형용사로 쓰이는 것

① 명사 뒤

The book on the table is about folk songs.
테이블위에 있는 책은 대중가요에 관한 것이다.

The cup of chocolate pudding went flying.
초콜릿 푸딩의 컵이 날아갔다.

② 주어 보충어

The spider man is in danger.
그 스퍼이더맨이 위험하다.

The workers were at recess.
그 노동자들이 휴식을 취했다.

③ 목적어 보충어

The president led the Korean peninsular in peace.
그 대통령은 한반도를 평화롭게 이끌었다.

Conflict between two Koreas makes the people in fear.
남북한 간의 갈등은 국민들을 불안하게 만든다.

B. 부사로 쓰이는 것

① 동사 수식

Birds fly in the sky.
새들이 하늘에서 난다.

A train runs through the tunnel.
열차가 터널을 통과하여 달린다.

② 형용사 수식

I'm sure of his success.
나는 그의 성공을 확신한다

The kids are good at English.
그 아이들은 영어를 잘한다.

Something was wrong with Andrea.
Andrea에 무엇인가가 잘못이 있었다.

③ 문장전체 수식

In Europe Michael goes to school.
After lunch we started our work.
We tiptoed into the library.
The light came in through the window.

유럽에서 마이클은 학교에 다닌다.
점심후에 우리는 우리의 일을 시작했다.
우리는 발끝으로 조심스럽게 도서관에 들어갔다.
불빛이 창문을 통해 들어왔다.

 확인문제 8

다음 각각 문장에서 밑줄 그은 '전치사+명사'가 형용사로 쓰였는지 부사로 쓰였는지를 말하시오.
그리고 각각 해석해보세요.

(01). Indians lived in this valley.

(02). The carriage goes down the road.

(03). Midas returned to the place.

(04). Everyone talked about the palace.

(05). There was no smile on his face.

(06). The sound of wheels approached along the road.

(07). From a distance, the rock looked like a human face.

(08). He spent his childhood in the log cabin.

(09). The sailors live in the small village by the sea.

(10). Do you know the Greek story of Midas?

〈정답과 해설 16P〉

to

전치사 to	to+동사원형

to는 전치사 to와 동사의 성격을 바꿔주는 'to 동사원형'이 있다. 완전히 다른 것이다.
'object to', 'look forward to', 'be used to(~에 익숙하다)', 'from A to B' 등에서 to는
전치사 to이다. 전치사 to다음에는 명사나 '동사원형ing'가 온다.

We object to moving the City Hall.   우리는 시청을 옮기는 것을 반대한다.
The kids look forward to going to school.   그 아이들은 학교에 가는 것을 학수고대한다.

'be going to'로 예를 들면,

be going to 동사원형	be going to 명사
~할 예정이다(=will)	~에 가고 있는 중이다
to는 'to 동사원형'	to는 전치사 to

be going to는 'to+동사원형'의 to와 '전치사 to'인 경우 두 가지 모두로 사용된다. 'to 동사
원형'으로 쓰인 'be going to 동사원형'은 '~할 예정이다'로 'will'로 바꿔 쓸 수 있다. 전치사
to로 쓰인 'be going to 명사'는 '~에 가고 있는 중이다'이다.

A. be going to 동사원형
'~ 할 예정이다'라는 뜻으로 will로 대신 쓸 수 있다.

She is going to do a lot of work.
   = She will do a lot of work.   그녀는 많은 일을 할 예정이다.
They are going to live in America.
   = They will live in America.   그들은 미국에서 살 예정이다.
We're going to read many books.
   = We will read many books.   우리는 많은 책을 읽은 예정이다.
I'm going to go to school next year.
   = I will go to school next year.   나는 내년에 학교에 갈 예정이다.

B. be going to 명사
'~에 가고 있는 중이다'의 뜻이고 여기에서 to는 전치사이다.

I'm going to school.   나는 학교에 가고 있는 중이다
She is going to the supermarket.   그녀는 수퍼마켓에 가고 있는 중이다.
The boys are going to the pool.   그 소년들은 수영장에 가고 있는 중이다.

다음 문장에서 사용된 'be going to'가 '～할 예정이다(will)'의 뜻으로 쓰인 것은 A, '～에 가고 있는 중이다'로 쓰인 것은 B로 쓰시오.

(01). We're going to the library.

(02). They are going to the party.

(03). I am going to clean my room.

(04). He is going to visit his grandparents.

(05). Ms. Park is going to drink tea.

(06). They were going to her grandmother's.

(07). My mom was going to the supermarket.

(08). The girls are going to the mountain.

(09). Smith is going to do his math homework.

(10). It is going to rain this afternoon.

《정답과 해설 16P》

Grammar in Reading

〈정답과 해설 16~17P〉

1. 다음 글의 빈칸에 알맞은 전치사를 각각 고르시오.

The train ⓐ (for, into) Washington came ⓑ (into, until) the station. A lot of people hurried ⓒ (with, into) the train. A young woman was sitting ⓓ (in, for)) the train. She was very beautiful. Two men came in and sat ⓔ (across, on) from her.

01. ⓐ-

02. ⓑ-

03. ⓒ-

04. ⓓ-

05. ⓔ-

2. 다음 글의 빈칸에 알맞은 전치사를 각각 쓰시오.

Claire: Can I go ⓐ _____ a science camp?

Fangin: Science camp? When is it?

Claire: It's ⓑ _____ June 5-7

Fangin: What are you going to do there?

Claire: We're going to learn about space and watch the stars ⓒ _____ night.

Fangin: All night, my son. Who's going ⓓ _____ you.

Claire: Our science teacher and some students ⓔ _____ the club.

Fangin: OK. you can go. Leave your teacher's phone number just in case.

Claire: I will, Thanks, Dad.

01. ⓐ-

02. ⓑ-

03. ⓒ-

04. ⓓ-

05. ⓔ-

Grammar in Reading

〈정답과 해설 17P〉

3. 다음 글의 빈칸에 알맞은 전치사를 각각 쓰시오.

ⓐ _____ our club, we take pictures ⓑ _____ people, places, and things. We sometimes go to parks and rivers ⓒ _____ photo trips. Going out ⓓ _____ a camera is a lot of fun! ⓔ _____ our school festival, we display our photos ⓕ _____ the hallway.

01. ⓐ-
02. ⓑ-
03. ⓒ-
04. ⓓ-
05. ⓔ-
06. ⓕ-

4. 다음 글의 빈칸에 알맞은 전치사를 각각 쓰시오.

Our club members try to turn their ideas ⓐ _____ cool inventions. Have you ever heard of an alarm pillow?

ⓑ _____ the morning, it will make you get up ⓒ _____ time. You will never be late for school again. This is one ⓓ _____ our club's coolest inventions. We have special activities, too. We sometimes participate ⓔ _____ invention contests. Last year, one of our club members won second prize in a big contest. Every September, we put the newest inventions ⓕ _____ display and invite friends and families to see them.

01. ⓐ-
02. ⓑ-
03. ⓒ-
04. ⓓ-
05. ⓔ-
06. ⓕ-

Grammar in Reading

〈정답과 해설 17~18P〉

5. 다음 글의 빈칸에 알맞은 전치사를 각각 쓰시오.

I go ⓐ _____ school everyday, but I do not go to school ⓑ _____ Sunday. I go to church on Sunday. I meet many friends at church. We do not study ⓒ _____ church. We pray to God at church. My father does not go to work on Sunday. He does not believe in God, and he does not go to church. My father likes to go fishing. I have a dog. It sleeps ⓓ _____ noon, but it does not sleep on Sunday until noon. It plays with me. My friends do not like dogs, and they do not play ⓔ _____ my dog. They play basketball. My family eats dinner out ⓕ _____ Sundays. We do not eat dinner ⓖ _____ home.

01. ⓐ-　　　　　　　　　　　　02. ⓑ-
03. ⓒ-　　　　　　　　　　　　04. ⓓ-
05. ⓔ-　　　　　　　　　　　　06. ⓕ-
07. ⓖ-

6. 다음 글의 빈칸에 알맞은 전치사를 각각 쓰시오.

Step 1. Take ten deep breaths. Breathe in slowly and deeply ⓐ _____ your nose, and then breathe out slowly ⓑ _____ your mouth.

Step 2. Roll your neck. Slowly roll your head ⓒ _____ a full circle. Repeat nine times.

Step 3. Stand and stretch. Stand up and stretch your hands high. ⓓ _____ your head. Hold your hands together and bend your body backwards. This exercise may help you to grow taller, too.

Step 4. Face your partner. Lift the corners of your mouth ⓔ _____ two fingers and smile widely. Look at your partner, but do not move your eyes for two minutes. This exercise will give you a nice smile.

Step 5. Relax. Sit ⓕ _____ a comfortable chair. Keep your hands at your sides. ⓖ _____ your head down to your toes, imagine each part ⓗ _____ your body and tell it to relax. Take your time.

01. ⓐ-　　　　　　　　　　　　02. ⓑ-
03. ⓒ-　　　　　　　　　　　　04. ⓓ-
05. ⓔ-　　　　　　　　　　　　06. ⓕ-
07. ⓖ　　　　　　　　　　　　08. ⓗ

〈정답과 해설 18P〉

1. 다음 각 문장에 들어갈 전치사를 보기에서 찾아 쓰시오.

on	at	in	since	between	until

01. What do you usually do _____ Sundays?

02. Miss. Smith was born _____ December, 1998.

03. The man was born _____ January 1, 1981.

04. The train got there _____ eight this morning.

05. His aunt went to America _____ February, 2011.

06. Fall arrived in Chicago _____ 12:37 on August 20, 2014.

07. Jack has studied Chinese in this school _____ the year of 2013.

08. Before 2003 there was no air line _____ the two cities.

09. The younger sister didn't go to bed _____ eleven last night.

10. Some shop often _____ 10 a.m. and 3:30 p.m. during the spring Festival.

2. 다음 문장의 빈칸에 알맞은 전치사를 보기에서 골라 쓰시오.

at	on	in	for	during	since	until	between	along	around	before	after

01. Lisa gets up ____ 7:00 everyday.

02. Leaves turn red and yellow _____ fall.

03. Wash you hands _____ dinner.

04. Korean eat Songpyeon _____ Chusok.

〈정답과 해설 18P〉

05. We have lunch at school _____ noon.

06. They'll go shopping _____ Sunday.

07. My sister does her homework _____ school.

08. My brother is usually at home _____ the winter.

09. The manager has been abroad _____ 2009.

10. Would you put these books ____ the table?

11. The moon moves _____ the earth.

12. There are many holidays and festivals _____ January.

13. These birds often follow ships at sea _____ days at a time.

14. A man has lived on the earth _____ almost one million years.

3. 다음 문장에서 잘못된 부분이 있는 문장을 찾아 올바로 고쳐 쓰시오.

01. Francisco is on the kitchen.

_____ → _____

02 The picture is hanging by the wall.

_____ → _____

03. There are 4 people at my family.

_____ → _____

04. Let's go shopping at the afternoon.

_____ → _____

05. It has been raining by noon.

_____ → _____

〈정답과 해설 18P〉

06. How many countries are there at Africa?
_____ → _____

07. My father met my mother first on a restaurant.
_____ → _____

08. She was happy for the vacation.
_____ → _____

09. They have not met each other from childhood.
_____ → _____

10. I will be back here until 5 o'clock.
_____ → _____

4. 다음 문장에서 두 개의 전치사 중 보다 적당한 것을 찾아 쓰시오.

01. Thick ice is on top (from, of) the water.

02. It is hard to move (at, on) deep snow.

03. Mike and Spike arrived (at, with) the site.

04. Now we can go up (to, from) our room.

05. People pick nuts (from, to) the trees.

06. We had birthday cake (of, for) breakfast.

07. Three crocodiles wake up (by, with) the sun.

08. Camels carry food and tents (on, in) their backs.

09. Mike will fly his kite (by, until) bedtime.

10. The beggars even looked (in, for) the trash can.

11. Wash your faces and put (at, on) clean clothes.

12. People in the Arctic dress (in, on) warm clothes.

13. The classmates found everywhere (to, for) the hamsters.

14. The little princess baked the cake (at, in) the oven.

15. Two ducks run down (with, to) the muddy, muddy swamp.

16. Three little monkeys and a crocodile sit (at, under) a tree.

17. The crocodiles push the old car to the top (of, over) the hill.

18. A hen, a duck and a goose put some berries (in, to) the basket.

19. The cook mixed everything together and put it (from, into) pans.

20. Two pigs and three dogs will hike at sunrise (at, on) a lovely and warm day.

memo.

Chapter

07

Noun Clause
명사절

명사절은 주어, 목적어, 보충어, 동격, 전치사 뒤에서 쓰인다.

- ◆ <u>that</u> 주어+동사
- ◆ <u>의문사</u> 주어+동사
- ◆ <u>wh-ever</u> 주어+동사
- ◆ <u>whether/if</u> 주어+동사
- ◆ <u>what</u> 주어+동사

Study 01 that절

~라는 것- that: 평서문(주장문)을 연결한다.

1. 주어- that절이 주어에 쓰이면 보통 가주어 it을 쓰고 that절을 뒤로 뺀다.

- <u>That she is honest</u>/ is certain.
  - → It is certain /<u>that she is honest</u>.

  그녀가 정직하다는 것은 확실하다.

- <u>That he will succeed in life</u>/ is uncertain.
  - → It is uncertain <u>that he will succeed in life</u>.

  그가 인생에서 성공할 것이라는 것은 불확실하다.

2. 목적어- 목적어 자리에서 접속사 that은 자주 생략된다.

- He said <u>(that) his wife needed a baby-sitter</u>.

  그는 그의 아내가 베이비시터가 필요하다고 말했다.

- Grandfather says <u>(that) we should take care of ourselves</u>.

  할아버지는 우리가 우리 자신을 돌봐야한다고 말한다.

- Can you believe <u>(that) these islands are sinking into the ocean</u>?

  너는 이 섬들이 큰 바다속으로 가라앉고 있다는 것을 믿을 수 있니?

- The scientists said <u>(that) someday the islands would disappear from the map</u>.

  과학자들은 어느 날 그 섬들이 지도에서 사라질 것이라고 말했다.

3. 주어보충어– 주어 보충어자리에서 that은 가끔 생략된다.

- The problem is (that) his family is very poor.   문제는 그의 가족이 가난하다는 것이다.
- The point is that Korea is the Republic of democracy.   핵심은 대한민국은 민주공화국이라는 것이다.

4. 동격

- The fact that she is liar is certain.(The fact = that she is liar)

                 그가 거짓말쟁이라는 사실은 확실하다.

5. 전치사 뒤

- The election is invalid in that the organizations of the government interfered with it.

               그 선거는 정부조직들이 선거에 개입했다는 점에서 무효다.

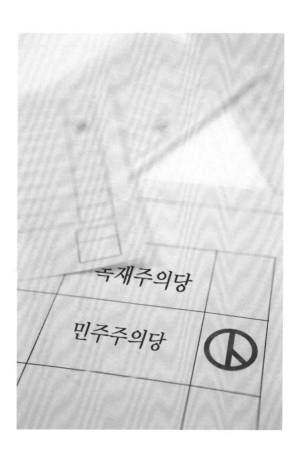

다음 문장에서 명사절을 밑줄 그으시오. 그리고 해석하시오.

(01). I think the design is all right.

→ _____

(02). I think that Mina will succeed.

→ _____

(03). I don't think the design looks that bad.

→ _____

(04). I think that soccer is the most exciting sport.

→ _____

(05). I know that Kevin's birthday party is this Saturday.

→ _____

(06). I think that Junsu has the best smile in our class.

→ _____

(07). I think teachers should allow us to use smart phones at school.

→ _____

〈정답과 해설 18~19P〉

🔍 확인문제 2

다음 두 문장을 연결하시오. 그리고 해석하시오.

(01). She is pretty + (   ) is true.

→ _____ , _____

(02). He will win the first prize + (   ) is possible.

→ _____ , _____

(03). We believe (   ) + He will get well.

→ _____ , _____

(04). People think (   ) + He is a crook.

→ _____ , _____

(05). The fact is (   ) + She is an idiot.

→ _____ , _____

(06). Our trouble is (   ) + We are short of water.

→ _____ , _____

〈정답과 해설 19P〉

Study **02**   whether/if 주어+동사~

~인지 어떤지– whether/if: 의문사 없는 의문문을 연결한다.

의문사 없는 의문문의 결합:

whether/if 다음에는 반드시 의문문 순서가 아니라 일반문장[주어+(조동사)+동사 ~] 순서로 써야 한다.

- I wonder + Is she a nurse?

→ I wonder whether/if she is a nurse.   나는 그녀가 간호사인지 어떤지 궁금하다.

★ do/does/did는 없어진다.

☞ do는 그냥 없어진다.

- I wonder + Do you want coffee?

→ I wonder whether/if you want coffee.   나는 네가 커피를 원하는지 어떤지 궁금하다.

☞ does는 없어지는 대신 동사원형에 -(e)s를 쓴다.

- They don't know + Does he work there?

→ They don't know whether/if he works there.   그들은 그가 거기에서 일하는 지 어떤지 모른다.

☞ did는 없어지는 대신 동사를 과거동사로 쓴다.

- I wonder + Did you meet your friend?

→ I wonder whether/if you met your friend?   나는 네가 너의 친구를 만났는지 궁금하다

1. 주어- whether절이 주어에 쓰이면 보통 가주어 it을 쓰고 whether절을 뒤로 뺀다.

- <u>Whether the baby is a son or a daughter</u>/ is uncertain.

  = It is uncertain <u>whether the baby is a son or a daughter</u>.

  아이가 아들인지 딸인지 불확실하다.

- <u>Whether he died or not</u> is known to the public.

  = It is known to the public <u>whether he died or not.</u>

  그가 죽었는지 죽지 않았는지 사람들에게 알려지지 않았다.

2. 목적어

- He asked Eric <u>whether/ if they could come back later</u>.

  그는 Eric에게 그들이 나중에 돌아 올 수 있는지를 물었다.

- Guard ants smell <u>whether/if we're a friend or a foe</u>.

  경비개미들은 우리가 친구인지 적인지 냄새 맡는다.

3. 주어보충어

- Her wonder is <u>whether he is a spy or a businessman</u>.

  그녀의 궁금함은 그가 스파이인지 비즈니스맨인지이다.

- The problem was <u>whether we will persuade the old man or not</u>.

  문제는 우리가 그 노인을 설득할 것인가 못할 것인가이다.

🔍 확인문제 3

다음 문장을 연결하시오.

(01). Will she come? + (   ) is his worry.

→ _____ , _____

(02). I wonder (   ) + Is he a crook?

→ _____ , _____

(03). Their worry is (   ) + will I pass the exam?

→ _____ _____ , _____

《정답과 해설 19P》

Study 03 의문사 덩어리 주어+동사~

의문사(who, what, when, where, how 등):의문사 있는 의문문을 연결한다.

의문사 있는 의문문의 결합:

반드시 의문사(덩어리) 일반문장[주어+(조동사)+동사~]순서로 써야 한다.

• Do you know + How old is she?

→ Do you know how old she is?   너는 그녀가 몇 살 먹었는지 아니?

• Please tell me + How can you make much money?

→ Please tell me how you can make much money.   나에게 네가 어떻게 많은 돈을 벌 수 있는지 말해 주세요.

★조동사 do, does, did는 없어진다.

☞ do는 그냥 없어진다.

• You don't know + What do they make?

→ You don't know what they make.   너는 그들이 무엇을 만드는지 모른다.

☞ does는 없어지는 대신 동사원형에 -(e)s를 붙인다.

• We don't know + Where does he live?

→ We don't know where he lives.   우리는 그가 어디에 사는지 모른다.

☞ 또 did는 없어지는 대신 동사를 과거동사로 쓴다.

• Mom wonders + What did you buy there?

→ Mom wonders what you bought there.   엄마는 네가 거기에서 무엇을 샀는지 궁금해 한다.

1. 주어

- <u>When she was born</u>/ doesn't matter.

  그녀가 언제 태어났는가는 중요하지 않다.

- <u>Who stole my bag</u> has not come out into the open.

  누가 나의 가방을 훔쳤는가가 밝혀지지 않았다.

2. 목적어

- I know <u>where those monkeys are from</u>.

  나는 저 원숭이들이 어디로부터 왔는지 안다.

- People wonder <u>when he will come back</u>.

  사람들은 그가 언제 올 것인지 궁금하다.

3. 주어 보충어

- The problem is <u>where he lives</u>.

  문제는 그가 어디에 사는가이다.

- The question is <u>how he will get a job</u>.

  문제는 어떻게 그가 직업을 구하는 가이다.

4. 동격

- We have a question, <u>where she gets the money</u>. (a question= where she gets the money)

  우리는 그녀가 돈을 어디서 구했는지에 대한, 한 가지 의문을 가지고 있다.

5. 전치사 뒤

- We got to <u>where it's warmer</u>.

  우리는 더 따뜻한 곳에 도착했다.

다음 두 문장을 연결하시오. 그리고 해석하시오.

(01). I know (   )+ What do you want?

→ _____,_____

(02). Tell me (   )+ How old is your dad?

→ _____,_____

(03). May I ask you (   )? + How tall is she?

→ _____,_____

(04). Do you know (   )?+ Where was he born?

→ _____,_____

(05). I wonder (   ). + What did you do last weekend?

→ _____,_____

(06). We don't know (   ) + When does your business start?

→ _____,_____

〈정답과 해설 19P〉

Study 04 what절: ~한 것- what(=the thing which)

1. 주어

- <u>What we need</u> is a computer expert to help us.

  우리가 필요한 것은 우리를 도울 컴퓨터 전문가이다.

- <u>What he says</u> is wrong.

  그가 말하는 것은 틀렸다.

2. 목적어

- He knows <u>what we say</u>.

  그는 우리가 말한 것을 안다.

- I can't understand <u>what he means</u>.

  나는 그가 의미하는 것을 이해할 수 없다.

3. 주어 보충어

- This is <u>what she says</u>.

  이것이 그녀가 말하는 것이다.

- Peace is <u>what we want</u>.

  평화가 우리가 원하는 것이다.

4. 전치사 뒤

- My pupils are good at <u>what I teach</u>.

  나의 학생들은 내가 가르치는 것을 잘한다.

- Kids are interested in <u>what a robot does</u>.

  아이들은 로봇이 행하는 것에 흥미가 있다.

다음 명사절을 찾아 밑줄 긋고 해석하시오.

(01). What the people want is freedom and peace.

→ _____

(02). This is what he wants to say.

→ _____

(03). I don't want what they have.

→ _____

〈정답과 해설 19P〉

Study 05 wh-ever절

~ 한 누구(어떤 것)이나- wh-ever

1. 주어

• Whoever is smart/ will be praised.

스마트한 사람 누구나 칭찬 받을 것이다.

• Whatever goes upon two legs/ is an enemy.

두발로 걷는 것들은 무엇이나 적이다.

2. 목적어

• Cam always remembers/ whatever she sees.

Cam은 항상 그녀가 본 것 무엇이나 기억한다.

3. 보충어

• What I want is/ whichever is cheap and has good quality.

내가 원하는 것은 싸고 품질 좋은 것 어떤 것이나이다.

확인문제 6

다음 명사절을 찾아 밑줄 긋고 해석하시오.

(01). I will do whatever she really wants.

→ _____

(02). I'll give you whatever you like for a birthday gift.

→ _____

(03). They will welcome whoever wants to come.

→ _____

《정답과 해설 19P》

Grammar in Reading

〈정답과 해설 19~20P〉

1. 아래 글에서 어법상 맞지 않는 것을 찾아 쓰시오.

We use credit cards a lot. We transfer money from account to account. Some people think whether coins and paper money may not be used in the future. What kind of money will take their place? We'll just have to wait and see.

답 (   )

2. 아래 글에서 접속사 that이 생략된 부분을 모두 찾아 쓰시오.

Asako : I guess you have a point there. By the way, I have a question. We usually pay individually in Japan. How come one person usually pays for everybody in Korea?

Kevin : Oh, I also thought that was very strange at first. I think the oldest person always picks up the bill.

MC　　: Well, you can consider it just a part of Korean culture.
However, it's changing these days. Many young people like to pay individually. We also take turns paying.

Kevin : I see. Anyway, I'm used to paying for my younger friends now.
When I went out with my American friends last weekend, I just picked up the bill for everybody. Now, they all love me.

MC　　: Ha ha ha. I guess you're almost Korean, Kevin. Well, our time is up. Thank you for all your interesting stories. Goodbye, everyone!

Grammar in Reading

〈정답과 해설 21P〉

3. 다음 글에서 (　　) 안에 알맞은 말을 쓰시오.

Today was my first day as a Green Kid. I started my first project day by taking the stairs instead of the elevator. I felt great because my small effort saved electricity. The only problem is ⓐ (　　) my apartment is on the 15th floor. I guess ⓑ (　　) I'd better not go out too often.

01. ⓐ

02. ⓑ

4. 아래 글에서 명사절을 모두 찾으시오.

Hello, everyone. My name is Opportunity, and I am a robot on Mars. NASA scientists sent me to explore Mars in 2003. Do you know why they sent me to Mars and not to a different planet? It is because Mars is similar to Earth. ˡMars and Earth have valleys and mountains. The two planets have similar weather and seasons.

Can you imagine how long it took me to get to Mars? It took me about 7 months to reach Mars. It was such a long trip! The distance from Earth to Mars changes all the time because the two planets are moving around the Sun at different speeds.

〈정답과 해설 21P〉

5. 다음 글에서 (   ) 안에 알맞은 말을 쓰시오.

Milo Cress says, "Our plastic straws will be around even after our grandchildren." He wants to save the Earth from straws. But how? He believes ⓐ (   ) it is simple. Just say, "No straw, please!" More and more people are following his lead.

Milo is a little boy ⓑ (   ) is only ten years old, but he is changing a big country like the USA.

01. ⓐ

02. ⓑ

6. 다음 문장에서 명사절을 모두 찾아 밑줄 그으시오. 그리고 그 명사절에서 생략된 접속사를 쓰시오.

I think I am a lucky boy. You know why, don't you? I have a loving family and friends. My dad spends a lot of time with me. We enjoy playing basketball together. We talk a lot and he always listens to me. I hope you are a good dad like my dad. I also hope you still keep in touch with Inho and Minsu. They are my best friends and I believe they are still your best friends.

〈정답과 해설 21P〉

1. 다음 <보기>와 같이 주어진 또 하나의 문장을 접속사 that을 사용하여 [   ]안에 넣어 한 문장으로 연결하시오. 그리고 각각 해석하시오.

> I heard [   ].
> You are leaving for Canada.
>
> → <u>I heard that you are leaving for Canada.</u>
>
> → <u>나는 네가 캐나다를 향하여 떠날 예정이라고 들었다.</u>

01. We know [   ].
    Yumi is Sujin's sister.

    → _____

    → _____

02. He thought [   ].
    She was going to cry.

    → _____

    → _____

03. They believe [   ].
    Her son is diligent.

    → _____

    → _____

04. The problem is [   ].
    Sue lost the key.

    → _____

    → _____

05. The fact is [   ].
    She doesn't like her new job.

    → _____

    → _____

〈정답과 해설 22P〉

06. The point is [   ].
We can't wait any longer.
→ _____
→ _____

07. [   ] is certain.
You will be a winner.
→ _____
→ _____

08. [   ] is important.
We should be honest and diligent.
→ _____
→ _____

09. [   ] is careless.
You have lost your wallet.
→ _____
→ _____

10. I believe [   ].
Planning is the most important thing for a trip.
→ _____
→ _____

2. 다음 문장에서 명사절을 찾아 밑줄을 그으시오. 그리고 해석하시오.

01. People wonder where Mickey worked.
→ _____ , _____

02. Do you know what the word means?
→ _____ , _____

03. She asked him if he did his homework.
→ _____ , _____

〈정답과 해설 22P〉

04. I wonder how you solved this problem.

→ _____ , _____

05. Mom asked me if I was fond of music.

→ _____ , _____

06. We think that you can solve this problem.

→ _____ , _____

07. Can you tell me if you're planning to come?

→ _____ , _____

08. I wonder if you understand the teacher's words.

→ _____ , _____

09. They wonder what the little Mouse is going to do.

→ _____ , _____

10. They don't know whether she is invited or not.

→ _____ , _____

11. Mom knows that you are unable to attend a meeting.

→ _____ , _____

12. The little Mouse knows how he should save the strawberry.

→ _____ , _____

13. Mother Bear asks Little Bear if he wants to wear a fur coat.

→ _____ , _____

14. Your friends wonder whether you can solve this problem or not.

→ _____ , _____

〈정답과 해설 22P〉

3. 다음 각각의 문장에서 명사절을 표시하시오. 그리고 해석하시오.

01. I will save what I have typed.
→ _____

02. What she wants is money.
→ _____

03. Eric said that he was ready.
→ _____

04. That she is a dictator is obvious.
→ _____

05. He didn't even say that he was sorry.
→ _____

06. He asked whether I would join the party.
→ _____

07. Whether he is a liar or not will be revealed.
→ _____

08. It is certain that Lee Sangho is a good reporter.
→ _____

09. Henry Baker told her that his name was Eric.
→ _____

10. You know that ants live and work together.
→ _____

11. I can't now remember if she has her car.
→ _____

12. The young girl asked me whether I could speak Spanish.
→ _____

〈정답과 해설 22~23P〉

13. I know that my mental camera doesn't need film.

→ _____

14. Whoever gets there first must wait for the others.

→ _____

15. I wonder where the real Corin lives.

→ _____

16. Robin Hood asked how old my father is.

→ _____

17. When the fire happened has not been revealed.

→ _____

18. How they enter the secret room is the police's doubt.

→ _____

19. The young don't understand the fact that society is corrupt.

→ _____

20. The important thing is that we take care of ourselves.

→ _____

4. 다음 우리말과 일치하도록 괄호 안에 주어진 단어를 배열하여 문장을 완성하시오.

01. 나는 그것이 멋진 건물이라고 생각한다.
→ I think _____.
(is, that, it, nice, building, a)

02. 그녀는 우리가 이틀 동안 거기에 머물 거라는 것을 알고 있다.
→ She knows _____.
(we, there, that, stay, will, for, two, days)

〈정답과 해설 23P〉

03. 준수는 미나가 가장 예쁜 소녀라고 믿는다.
    → Junsu believes _____.
        (the, Mina, girl, is, that, prettiest)

04. 그녀가 다시 올 것인지를 물어봐라.
    → Ask _____.
        (she, coming, if, back, is)

05. 그 설교자는 그가 그의 아내로 Sarah를 맞을지 묻는다.
    → The preacher asks _____.
        (have, whether, will, he, for, Sarah, his wife)

06. 그들은 내가 열심히 공부해야 한다고 생각한다.
    → They think _____.
        (that, should, study, I, harder)

07. 그들은 계획이 필수적이가고 생각한다.
    → They think _____.
        (planning, essential, that, is)

08. 그 남자는 전기가 가장 중요하다고 생각한다.
    → The man thinks _____.
        (that, the, electricity, is, most, important)

09. Telsa는 보다 많은 사람들이 전력을 사용할 수 있을 것이라고 믿었다.
    → Tesla believed _____.
        (use, people, that, could, electrical, more, power)

10. 우리는 그 언어를 배우는 것이 가장 필수적이라고 생각한다.
    → We think _____.
        (learning, the language, that, necessary, is, most)

Chapter

08

Adjective Clause
형용사절

형용사절은 명사 뒤에서 앞에 있는 명사를 꾸며준다.

접속대명사	사 람	who(=that)	whose	whom(=that)
	사 물	which(=that)	whose	which(=that)
접 속 부 사	때	when	장소	where	이유	why	방법	how

Study 01 접속(관계)대명사

	주어대신	소유격대신	목적어대신–생략가능
사 람	who(=that)	whose	whom(=that)–생략가능
사 물	which(=that)	whose	which(=that)–생략가능

접속대명사는 접속사 역할과 대명사 역할을 동시에 한다. 접속대명사 자신은 접속사 역할과 대명사 역할을 한다. 다만 그 접속대명사가 이끄는 절은 앞의 명사를 꾸며주는 형용사역할을 한다.

1. 사람

① 주어– who(=that)

• Look at the boy who[=that] is playing the violin.

바이올린을 연주하고 있는 소년을 보아라.

• Robinson asked one of the people who[=that] worked in the store.

로빈슨은 가게에서 일하는 사람들 중 한명에게 물었다.

② 목적어– whom (=that): 생략 가능

- Do you know the girl <u>whom[=that] I met yesterday</u>?

　　　　　　　　　　　　　너는 내가 어제 만난 소녀를 아느냐?

③ 소유격– whose

- Did you meet the travellers <u>whose bus was waiting in the street</u>?

　　　　　　　　너는 거리에서 버스가 기다리고 있는 여행객들을 만났느냐?

2. 사물

① 주어– which (=that)

- You wouldn't believe the crazy things <u>which[=that] happen in Mr.Frizzle's class</u>.
  너는 Frizzle씨의 수업에서 일어나는 열광적인 것들을 믿지 못할 것이다.

- A bulletin is a news report <u>which[=that] talks about very recent and importing events</u>.
  게시물은 매우 최근의 그리고 중요한 사건들에 관하여 말하는 뉴스이다.

② 목적어– which (=that): 생략 가능

- Have you seen the notice <u>which[=that] I posted last month</u>?

　　　　　　　　　　너는 내가 지난달에 포스트한 고지를 보았느냐?

③ 소유격– whose

- That is the car <u>whose comfort is very excellent</u>.

　　　　　　　　저것이 승차감이 좋은 차이다.

3. that만 사용하는 경우

- 사람과 사물(사람이 아닌 것)이 동시에 온 경우

- 전부(all, every 명사, everything, everybody 등)

- 전무(nothing, nobody, no 명사 등)

- 특정하는 표현들(the very, the same, the only 명사)

- the 최상급/ the 서수 등

① 사람과 사물(사람이 아닌 것)이 동시에 올 때
- I saw the girl and her kitten <u>that were playing in the park</u>.

나는 공원에서 놀고 있는 소녀와 그녀의 고양이를 보았다.

② 전부
- The man knows everything <u>(that) his son has done</u>.

그 남자는 그의 아들이 해온 모든 것을 안다.

③ 전무
- The police know nothing <u>(that) the robber has done</u>.

경찰은 강도가 행한 어떤 것도 모른다.

④ 특정
- The queen ant is the only ant <u>that lays eggs</u>.

여왕개미는 알을 낳는 유일한 개미다.

확인문제 1

다음 빈칸에 who 또는 which를 쓰시오.

(01). This is the woman _____ made the song.

(02). There is a tree _____ has many yellow leaves.

(03). The boy _____ is tall and handsome is my son.

(04). She sat on the chair _____ had a broken leg.

(05). The river _____ flows through London is the Thames.

(06). The couple need a woman _____ can take care of their baby.

(07). The picture _____ was hanging on the wall is very wonderful.

(08). Anybody _____ went to the party really were happy to see many friends.

《정답과 해설 23P》

확인문제 2

다음 괄호 안에서 알맞은 것을 고르시오.

(01). This is the bird (who/ which) can speak.

(02). A thief is a person (that/ which) steals things.

(03). Ann needs a person (which/ that) is diligent and kind.

(04). The man (that/ which) opened the door was wearing a blue cap.

(05). The girl (which/ that) is standing next to the window is my cousin.

(06). I have a friend [who/ whose] father runs a business in L.A.

(07). Annie was the only one [which/ that] trusted me.

(08). This is the book [who/ which] would be easy for you.

(09). Once upon a time, there lived a girl [who/ whose] name was Gretel.

(10). Kate is an American girl [who/ whose] mother is a Korean.

《정답과 해설 23P》

다음 문장에서 형용사절에 밑줄 그으시오. 그리고 그 형용사절의 꾸밈을 받는 명사를 동그라미 하시오.
그리고 해석하시오.

(01). We thank all those who protect us.

   → _____

(02). The cat is a pet whose eyes seem very smart.

   → _____

(03). June 25 is the day when the war broke out.

   → _____

(04). Here is the book that I was just talking about.

   → _____

(05). A bay is an area near the ocean where the land goes inward.

   → _____

(06). Sarah kissed us all, even my father, who looked frightened.

   → _____

(07). I remembered another time when a wagon had taken Mama away.

   → _____

(08). My sister is a designer whose works are popular to the Asians.

   → _____

designer

〈정답과 해설 23P〉

확인문제 4

다음 두 문장을 괄호 안에 주어진 접속(관계)대명사를 이용하여 한 문장으로 만드시오. 그리고 해석하시오.

(01). This is the bird. It can speak.

→ _____ , _____

(02). Ann is the girl. She is diligent and kind.

→ _____ , _____

(03). This is the book. It is easy for you.

→ _____ , _____

(04). There are trees. My grandmother grew them.

→ _____ , _____

(05). I saw a cat. Mike played with it.

→ _____ , _____

(06). A thief is a person. He steals things.

→ _____ , _____

(07). Look at the pictures. They are on the wall.

→ _____ , _____

(08). This is the woman. She made the song.

→ _____ , _____

(09). I met the girl. I gave her the gift.

→ _____ , _____

(10). The woman is my aunt. She is working with me.

→ _____ , _____

〈정답과 해설 23P〉

Study 02   접속(관계)부사

앞명사를 부사로 받으면서 연결하는 접속부사. 즉 접속사 역할과 부사 역할을 동시에 한다.

때– when	장소– where	이유– why	방법– how

다만 the way와 how는 절대 같이 사용할 수 없다. the way와 how 중 하나를 생략하거나,
how 대신에 that을 사용하여 the way that으로 사용할 수 있다.

1. when – 때

- February is the month **when schools end**.   2월은 학교가 끝나는 달이다.
- 1960 is the year **when the pro–domocracy Movement of April 19th happened**.

  1960년은 4.19민주의거가 발생한 해이다.

2. where – 장소

- A refuge is a place **where you go to be safe**.   피난처는 네가 안전하기 위하여 가는 장소다.
- A castle is a place **where royalty usually lives**.   성은 보통 왕족이 사는 곳이다.

3. why – 이유

- Think of the reason **why you took mistakes in the test**.

  네가 시험에서 실수한 이유에 관하여 생각해 봐라.

4. how -방법

- We can't know (~~the way~~) how[=that] the prisoner escaped.

  우리는 그 죄수가 도망간 방법을 알 수 없다.

  ※주의) the way how는 함께 쓰이지 않는다. 대신 the way that은 사용된다.

🔍 확인문제 5

다음 문장을 접속부사 – when, where, why, how, that–로 연결하시오. 또 해석하시오.

(01). This is the town. He works there.

→ _____

(_____)

(02). Do you know the day? The new semester will start then.

→ _____

(_____)

(03). This is the way. He made much money by the way.

→ _____

(_____)

(04). They wonder the reason. He is late for the meeting for the reason.

, _____

(_____)

〈정답과 해설 24P〉

Grammar in Reading

〈정답과 해설 24P〉

1. 다음 빈칸에 알맞은 말을 넣으시오.

I was surprised to see that Mr. Portokalos smiled and congratulated me. He said, "The person ( ) gets the lucky slice with the coin will have good luck for the year." So I was really happy at that moment.

정답- ( )

2. 다음 빈칸에 알맞은 말을 넣으시오.

Today was Club Activity Day. I told my doll-making club members about the children ⓐ ( ) I met two weeks ago.

We decided to put on a puppet show for them. We started making the dolls ⓑ ( ) we will use in the show. We promised to practice for our puppet show on Mondays and Wednesdays. The more we practice, the better our show will be.

01. ⓐ- 　　　　　　　　　　　　　　02. ⓑ-

3. 다음 글에서 ( ) 안에 알맞은 말을 쓰시오.

Yesterday, I saw a documentary on TV. It was about a man ( ) tried to live without doing any harm to the environment. After watching it, I decided to start my own project, "Project Green Kid."

정답- ( )

4. 다음 글에서 (   ) 안에 알맞은 말을 쓰시오.

About 3,000 years ago in Italy, there was a small village (   ) grew into the powerful Roman Empire. It left a great heritage for us. How did these powerful Romans live their daily lives?

정답-(   )

5. 다음 글에서 (   ) 안에 알맞은 말을 쓰시오.

A champion is a winner,
A hero ...
Someone ⓐ (   ) never gives up.
Even when the going gets rough.
A champion is a member of
A winning team ...
Someone ⓑ (   ) overcomes challenges,
Even when it requires creative solutions,
A champion is an optimist,
A hopeful spirit ...
Someone ⓒ (   ) plays the game,
Even when the game is called life ...

01. ⓐ-   02. ⓑ-
03. ⓒ-

Grammar in Reading

〈정답과 해설 25~26P〉

6. 다음 글에서 (   ) 안에 알맞은 말을 쓰시오.

"After that, I don't know what happened to the Jewish woman. This is my daughter ⓐ (   )
I got that day." The old lady was silent for a moment, and then continued. "At first, she didn't
stop crying and I didn't know what to do.
I just kept trying my best to make her happy. However, she didn't enjoy talking to me for some
time. One day, my daughter surprised me with a Mother's Day present.

It was when she was six years old. She gave me a paper flower and a cute card ⓑ (   )
said, 'Happy Mother's Day.' It was a very special day. She always makes me so happy and I
love to hear her sweet little voice when she says, 'Hi, Mom.'"When we arrived at the airport, a
pretty lady ⓒ (   ) looked like the girl in the photo was waiting for her mom.
"Mom! Hi, Mom, here...."

01. ⓐ-   02. ⓑ-

03. ⓒ-

〈정답과 해설 26P〉

1. 빈칸에 알맞은 접속(관계)대명사를 쓰시오.

01. This is the gift _____ I will give Mina.

02. That is the car _____ I wanted to buy.

03. The book _____ Miso is reading is Minsu's.

04. The boy _____ broke the window ran away.

05. I saw the girl _____ my best friend loves.

06. There is a glass _____ is full of hot water.

07. This is the novel _____ she wrote last year.

08. She wanted to buy the dress _____ has a red ribbon.

09. The bike _____ my father bought for me was stolen.

10. The girl _____ is running around the playground is my student.

11. It is the most boring movie _____ I have ever seen.

12. There are a boy and a dog _____ are running in the playground.

2. 다음 문장에서 형용사절에 밑줄 그으시오. 그리고 그 형용사절의 꾸밈을 받는 명사를 동그라미 하시오. 그리고 해석하시오.

01. The door led right into a large kitchen, which was full of smoke.
→ _____ _____ _____

02. The Celts, who once lived in Ireland, celebrated the arrival of winter.
→ _____

〈정답과 해설 26P〉

03. The horizon is the place where the sky looks like it meets the ground.
→ _____

04. An anniversary is a day when people celebrates something from the past.
→ _____

05. The man is the professor whose university is very famous for engineering.
→ _____

06. Look at the park where many people stand together and take a picture.
→ _____

07. They saw live insects, mice, and chickens that were kept in the kitchen to feed the snakes, lizards, and alligators.
→ _____

3. 다음 두 문장을 한 문장으로 연결할 때 빈칸에 알맞은 접속(관계)부사 when, where, why, how, that 중 하나를 골라 쓰시오.

01. Seoul is the city. I live there.
→ Seoul is the city _____ I live.

02. 2016 is the year. I entered middle school then.
→ 2016 is the year _____ I entered middle school.

03. This is the place. They found the lost purse here.
→ This is the place _____ they found the lost purse.

04. Someone called me at the time. I was watching TV then.
→ Someone called me at the time _____ I was watching TV.

05. They don't know the reason. He went there for the reason.
→They don't know the reason _____ He went there.

〈정답과 해설 26P〉

06. England is the country. Shakespeare was born there.

→ England is the country ＿＿＿＿＿＿ Shakespeare was born.

07. I want to visit a town. The artist was born and raised there.

→ I want to visit a town ＿＿＿＿＿＿ the artist was born and raised.

08. The students understand the way. The teacher solved the question by the way.

→The students understand the way ＿＿＿＿＿＿ the teacher solved the question.

09. Would you recommend a restaurant? We can have nice seafood there.

→ Would you recommend a restaurant ＿＿＿＿＿＿ we can have nice seafood?

10. On May, the weather was so bad that we couldn't do anything. We went to the area then.

→ On May ＿＿＿＿＿＿ we went to the area, the weather was so bad that we couldn't do anything.

4. 다음 두 문장을 접속(관계)부사를 이용하여 한 문장으로 바꾸시오.

01. The children like the winter.
It snows a lot then.

→ ＿＿＿＿＿＿＿＿＿＿＿＿＿＿＿＿＿＿＿＿＿＿＿＿＿

02. This is the way.
He runs the company in this way.

→ ＿＿＿＿＿＿＿＿＿＿＿＿＿＿＿＿＿＿＿＿＿＿＿＿＿

03. This is the house.
He was born there.

→ ＿＿＿＿＿＿＿＿＿＿＿＿＿＿＿＿＿＿＿＿＿＿＿＿＿

04. He arrived at the palace.
The king lived there.

→ ＿＿＿＿＿＿＿＿＿＿＿＿＿＿＿＿＿＿＿＿＿＿＿＿＿

〈정답과 해설 26~27P〉

05. I don't know the reason.
    You bought a doll for the reason.

    → _____

06. The school is short of the space.
    The children can play safely there.

    → _____

5. 다음 우리말과 같은 의미가 되도록 괄호 안의 단어를 바르게 배열하여 문장을 완성하시오.

01. 그는 영국에서 온 내 친구이다.
    (from, my friend, England, he, is, who, is).

    → _____

02. 캥거루는 호주에 사는 동물이다.
    (lives, is, which, a kangaroo, in Australia, an animal).

    → _____

03. 그는 러시아에서 사는 친구가 한 명 있다.
    (Russia, lives, who, a, He, has, in, friend)

    → _____

04. 나는 나를 저녁식사에 초대한 남자를 만났다.
    (I, the, who, me, to, met, man, dinner, invited).

    → _____

05. 환하게 웃게 있는 그 노부인이 나의 엄마였다.
    (old, the, brightly, is, smiling, lady, who, mother, was, my).

    → _____

〈정답과 해설 27P〉

6. 다음 우리말에 맞도록 괄호 안에 주어진 단어들을 적절하게 나열하시오.

01. 미소가 읽고 있는 책은 민수의 것이다.
(book, Miso, reading, Minsu's, is, the, which, is)
→ _____

02. 창문을 깬 소년이 달아났다.
(broke, ran away, the boy, the window, who)
→ _____

03. 이것은 내가 Mina에게 줄 선물이다.
(gift, will, I, Mina, is, this, the, that, give)
→ _____

04. 저것은 내가 사고 싶었던 차이다.
(the car, that, which, is, I, to, buy, wanted)
→ _____

05. 이것은 그녀가 지난해에 쓴 소설이다.
(wrote, which, this, she, is, the novel, last, year)
→ _____

06. 뜨거운 물로 가득 찬 잔이 있다.
(of, is, full hot, there, is, a glass, which, water)
→ _____

07. 나의 아버지가 나를 위하여 사준 자전거가 도난당했다.
(my father, bought, the bike, was, stolen, which, for, me)
→ _____

08. 운동장 주변을 달리고 있는 소녀는 나의 학생이다.
(playground, is, running, the girl, who, around, is, my student, the)
→ _____

memo.

Chapter

09

Adverb Clause
부사절

문장 전체를 꾸며주는 부사절

문장 맨 앞이나 맨 뒤, 혹은 중간에서 문장 전체를 꾸며준다.

Study 01 때를 나타내는 부사절
when/ while/ after/ before/ until/ as soon as

1. when: ～할 때

> When 주어 +동사 ～, 주어 +동사 ～.
>
> (= 주어 +동사～ when 주어 +동사 ～)

- When I get up in the morning, I feel good.　　　　나는 아침에 일어날 때, 나는 기분이 좋다.
  = I feel good when I get up in the morning.

- When Cam was younger, people called her Jennifer.

  　　　　　Cam이 더 어렸을 때, 사람들은 그녀를 Jennifer라고 불렀다.

- When the cat is away, the mice will play.　　　　고양이가 없는 곳에 쥐들이 판을 벌린다.

- Grandfather took care of me when my mother died.

  　　　　　나의 엄마가 돌아가셨을 때, 할아버지가 나를 돌보았다.

다음 when으로 연결된 부사절에 밑줄 긋고 해석하시오.

(01). You can go when the bell rings.

→ _____

(02). When I have a cold, I drink orange juice.

→ _____

(03). Ask your mother when you should open the door.

→ _____

(04). When I was in school, we didn't have computers.

→ _____

(05). I'll show you the garden when it stops raining.

→ _____

(06). When you are tired, you should go home early.

→ _____

(07). You should raise your hand when you call for a taxi.

→ _____

(08). When you eat something, you should wear a napkin.

→ _____

(09). The dog always barks when anyone comes near the house.

→ _____

(10). You should say hello to each other when you meet someone.

→ _____

《정답과 해설 27P》

다음 2개의 문장을 접속사 when을 사용하여 한 문장으로 연결하시오.

> I took a walk on the street. I met my best friend.
> → When I took a walk on the street, I met my best friend.
> OR I met my best friend when I took a walk on the street.

(01). George loved history. He was at school.

→ _____

OR _____

(02). The kids don't go out. It snows.

→ _____

OR _____

(03). We helped him. He could finish his work earlier.

→ _____

OR _____

(04). The boys heard the sad news. They cried.

→ _____

OR _____

(05). My sister is angry. She wants to be alone.

→ _____

OR _____

(06). The children feel good. They sing a song.

→ _____

OR _____

(07). The program was over. I turned off the TV.

→ _____

OR _____

(08). They got to the hotel. There was no room.

→ _____

OR _____

〈정답과 해설 27P〉

2. while: ~하는 동안 & ~ 한 반면에

While 주어 +동사 ~, 주어 +동사 ~.
(= 주어+동사~ while 주어 +동사 ~)

- Cam waited while Eric rested.　　　　　　Eric이 쉬는 동안에 Cam은 기다렸다.
- While most women stayed at home with their children, she traveled the world.
  대부분의 여성들이 그들의 아이들과 집에 머무는 반면에 그녀는 세계를 여행했다.

확인문제 3

다음 2개의 문장을 접속사 while을 사용하여 한 문장으로 연결하시오.

> I hope to see One Direction. I am there.
> → While I am there, I hope to see One Direction.
> OR I hope to see One Direction while I am there.

(01). My parents were fighting each other. I watched the TV.

　　　→ _____

　　　OR _____

(02). The boys were playing baseball. The girls drew pictures.

　　　→ _____

　　　OR _____

(03). She was waiting for the bus. She read the magazine.

　　　→ _____

　　　OR _____

(04). George was in the library. His uncle visited his house.

　　　→ _____

　　　OR _____

(05). Mom was cooking. I studied English Listening.

→ _____

OR _____

(06). His parents were out. He saw a movie.

→ _____

OR _____

〈정답과 해설 28P〉

🔍 확인문제 4

다음 주어진 문장을 바르게 해석하시오.

(01). I like sports while he likes music.

→ _____

(02). Some people like juice while others don't.

→ _____

(03). I listened to music while I was waiting for you.

→ _____

(04). Don't disturb him while he is studying.

→ _____

(05). He spent most of his time while his wife worked hard.

→ _____

(06). He played outside while his mother was cooking dinner.

→ _____

〈정답과 해설 28P〉

3. after: ~한 후에/ before: ~ 전에

⊙ after
- I got my first gift after I arrived at Paris.
  = After I arrived at Paris, I got my first gift.

  내가 파리에 도착한 후 첫 번째 선물을 샀다.
- The show finished after he arrived.
  = After he arrived, the show ended.

  그가 도착한 뒤 공연이 끝났다.

⊙ before
- Don't cry before you are hurt.
  = Before you are hurt, don't cry.

  상처입기 전에 울지 마라.
- Next time, knock before you enter!
  = Next time, before you enter, knock!

  다음에 네가 들어가기 전에 노크해라.

🔍 확인문제 5

before와 after에 유념하여 다음 문장을 해석하시오.

(01). Won't you have another drink before you go?

　　　→ _____

(02). Please set the alarm clock before you go to bed.

　　　→ _____

(03). After Maria finished her homework, she watched television.

　　　→ _____

(04). Her father went to bed after he had washed the dishes.

　　　→ _____

(05). Andrew joined the club a year before he moved to the city.

　　　→ _____

(06). I told you not to eat a hotdog before you did that.

　　　→ _____

〈정답과 해설 28P〉

4. by the time: ～ 할 쯤 / whenever: - ～할 때마다(=every time, each time)

- By the time she was ten, she was handling her father's rifle with ease.

  그녀가 10살 먹을 쯤, 그녀는 그녀의 아버지의 장총을 쉽게 다루고 있었다.

- Billy smiles whenever Mr.Cooper looks at him.

  Cooper씨가 그를 볼 때 마다 Billy는 웃는다.

- Whenever my father sees an alligator, he says, "Just look at those teeth!"

  나의 아버지가 악어를 볼 때마다 그는 "단지 저 이빨을 봐" 라고 말한다.

 확인문제 6

다음 (   ) 안에 각각 알맞은 말을 아래 보기에서 골라 넣으시오.

| by the time | whenever |

(01). The roof leaks (   ) it rains.

(02). (   ) she arrived, most of the guests had left.

(03). (   ) we get there, the bank will be closed.

(04). (   ) I saw her, I thought my dad looked like her.

(05). (   ) she sees me, she always smiles.

〈정답과 해설 28P〉

5. until: ~할 때 까지

- I would like to wait until something nice happens.

  나는 멋진 어떤 일이 일어 날 때까지 기다리고 싶다.

- He worked until he was too tired to do more.

  그는 지쳐서 더 이상 일 할 수 없을 때 까지 일했다.

🔍 확인문제 7

다음 문장에서 until에 유념하여 우리말로 해석하시오.

(01). Leave the disk in drive A until the wizard is complete.

→ _____

(02). Stop your big talk until you show us some proof.

→ _____

(03). I didn't even know what was happening until it happened.

→ _____

〈정답과 해설 28P〉

6. as soon as 주어+동사(= on 동사원형ing) : ~하자마자

- As soon as I sat down to write a diary, the telephone rang.
  = On my sitting down to write a diary, the telephone rang.

  내가 일기를 쓰기 위하여 앉자마자 전화가 울렸다.

- As soon as Mary read the memo, she called someone.
  = On reading the memo, Mary called someone.   Mary가 그 메모를 읽자마자 누군가에게 전화했다.

- As soon as the boy saw a police officer, he ran away.
  = On seeing a police officer, the boy ran away.   그 소년이 경찰관을 보자마자 그는 도망갔다.

 확인문제 8

다음 우리말에 맞게 괄호안의 단어를 바르게 배열하시오.

(01). 그녀가 나를 보자마자 pinky는 씩 웃었다.

(As, she, saw, as, soon, me)

→ _____, Pinky grinned.

(02). 그 노인은 차에 타자마자 낮잠을 잤다.

(as, car, on, he, the, soon, as, got)

→The old man took a nap, _____.

(03). Michael이 집에 도착하자마자 축구 경기를 보기 위해 TV를 켰다.

(Michael, home, As, got, soon, as)

→ _____, he turned on TV to watch a soccer game.

(04). 우리의 이글루가 세워지자마자, 우리는 되돌아와 운동했다.

(our, As, igloo, was, as, soon, built)

→ _____, we went back to exercising.

(05). 내가 방에 들어가자마자 나의 누이가 나를 공격했다.

(I, soon, as, walked, into, the, As, room)

→ _____, my sister attacked me.

(06). 그녀의 딸은 숙제를 끝마치자마자, 컴퓨터 게임을 했다.

(As, the, finished, her, soon, daughter, as, homework)

→ _____, she played a computer game.

〈정답과 해설 28P〉

Study **02** 조건을 나타내는 부사절
if/ Once/ unless/ 명령문

1. if: ~한다면

- If you move, the picture will be blur.
- If you love me, set me free

네가 움직이면 사진이 흐릴 것이다.
그대가 날 사랑한다면 나를 자유롭게 해주세요.

CF 명사절에서 if - '~인지 어떤지'의 뜻으로 whether와 같다.
보통 목적어자리에서 사용된다.

- I wonder if she is a single or married.
  나는 그녀가 싱글인지 결혼했는지 궁금하다.

🔍 확인문제 9

다음 if절을 명사절과 부사절로 구별하시오. 그리고 해석하시오.

(01). I wonder if she will come here.

(02). Anyone will go there if you go.

(03). They don't know if his word is right.

(04). We can't decide if he is guilty.

(05). If you want to get a good grade, you must study hard.

(06). If the actress plays the main role, the movie will be a big success.

〈정답과 해설 28~29P〉

다음 if로 연결된 문장에서 부사절 if절에 밑줄하고 해석하시오.

(01). If it rains tomorrow, I will stay home.

→ _____

(02). If I get a good grade, I will be so happy.

→ _____

(03). If you see Tom, please call me at once.

→ _____

(04). If school finishes today, I will play baseball.

→ _____

(05). If I go to Paris, I will visit the Eiffel Tower.

→ _____

(06). If you practice hard, your mom will be happy.

→ _____

(07). We will start to play soccer, if the rain stops.

→ _____

(08). If it is sunny this Sunday, we will go on a picnic.

→ _____

(09). If you leave me now, you'll take away the biggest part of me.

→ _____

(10). Winter in Wyiming can be the most beautiful time of the year, if you are ready for it.

→ _____

〈정답과 해설 29P〉

2. Once: 일단 ～하면

- Once my mom starts talking, she doesn't shut up.

  그녀는 한 번 말을 시작하면 멈추질 않는다.

- It'll be a masterpiece once you have done the artwork.

  일단 그 예술 작품을 끝내기만 하면 대단한 작품이 될 것이다.

확인문제 11

다음 문장에서 once에 유념하여 우리말로 해석하시오.

(01). Once he starts to drink, he drinks five bottles.

→ _____

(02). Once you sign in, you should do your duty.

→ _____

(03). Once you decide, you must stick with it.

→ _____

(04). Once a beaver is two years old, it leaves the family.

→ _____

(05). Once she confirms the designs, we can begin production.

→ _____

〈정답과 해설 29P〉

3. unless(if ～ not)： ～하지 않는 다면

• You can't see the funguses unless you use a really powerful microscope.

네가 정말로 강력한 현미경을 사용할 수 없다면 곰팡이를 볼 수 없다.

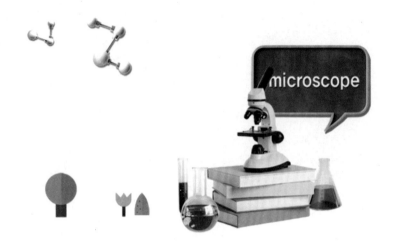

🔍 확인문제 12

다음 (　　　)안에 알맞은 말을 넣으시오.

(01). Continue to try steadily (　　　　) you succeed.

= 네가 성공할 때까지 계속하여 꾸준히 노력해라.

(02). (　　　　) you are in danger, don't call me.

= 네가 위험에 처하지 않는다면 나에게 전화하지 마세요.

(03). (　　　　) it rains tomorrow, I will go on a picnic.

= 내일 비가 내리지 않는다면 소풍 갈 것이다.

(04). (　　　　) you don't want to go, you may stay here.

= 네가 가기를 원치 않는다면 여기에 머물러도 된다.

〈정답과 해설 29P〉

Study 03   명령문, and(or)~

1. 명령문(동사원형), and 주어 will 동사원형 ~

> 명령문(동사원형) ~, and you can/will 동사원형 ~. :
> → If + you + 동사원형(be-are) ~, S can/will 동사원형~,
> ~해라, 그러면 S는 ~할 것이다.

- Knock, and the door will open.   노크해라, 그러면 문이 열릴 것이다.
  - → If you knock, the door will open.
- Be kind, and they will be kind to you.   친절해라, 그러면 그들이 네게 친절할 것이다.
  - → If you are kind, they will be kind to you.

🔍 확인문제 13

다음 문장을 If로 시작하여 다시 쓰시오.

(01). Seek, and you will get the thing.

→ _____

(02). Walk everyday, and you will be healthy.

→ _____

(03). Work hard, and you can achieve your dream.

→ _____

〈정답과 해설 29P〉

두 문장의 의미가 같도록 빈 칸에 알맞은 말을 쓰시오.

(01). If you get up early, you won't be late.

= Get up early, _____ you won't be late.

(02) If you take exercise, you will be healthy.

= Take exercise, _____ you will be healthy.

(03) If you aren't careful, you'll be in danger.

= Be careful, _____ you'll be in danger.

(04). If you are patient, you'll meet her soon.

= Be patient, _____ you'll meet her soon.

(05). If you lose weight, you will look great.

= Lose weight, _____ you will look great.

(06) If you eat crabs, you will stay thin forever.

= Eat crabs, _____ you will stay thin forever.

(07) If you study hard, you will pass the exam.

=Study hard, _____ you will pass the exam.

(08) If you learn English, you will succeed in the future.

= Learn English, _____ you will succeed in the future.

〈정답과 해설 29P〉

2. 명령문(동사원형) ~, or you will 동사원형~

> 명령문(동사원형) ~, or you will 동사원형 ~ :
>
> = If you don't 동사원형(혹은 be-aren't) ~, you will 동사원형 ~.
>
> = Unless you 동사원형(혹은 be-are) ~, you will 동사원형 ~.
>
> ~해라, 그렇지 않으면 ~할 것이다.

- Get up early, or you will be late again.　　　　일찍 일어나라, 그렇지 않으면 너는 다시 늦을 것이다.
  - → If you don't get up early, you will be late again.
  - → Unless you get up early, you will be late again.
- Take a taxi, or you'll miss the train.　　　　택시를 타거라, 그렇지 않으면 열차를 놓칠 것이다.
  - → If you don't take a taxi, you'll miss the train.
  - → Unless you take a taxi, you'll miss the train.

🔍 확인문제 15

다음 문장을 if와 unless로 시작하는 문장을 각각 쓰시오.

(01). Be ready now, or you will fail in the exam.

　　→ If _____

　　→ Unless _____

(02). Hurry up, or you won't catch the first train.

　　→ If _____

　　→ Unless _____

〈정답과 해설 29P〉

🔍 확인문제 16

두 문장의 의미가 같도록 빈 칸에 알맞은 말을 쓰시오.

(01). If you don't run fast, you can't catch the first train.

　　= Run fast, _____ you can't catch the first train.

(02) If you don't start now, you will miss the bus.

　　= Start now, _____ you won't miss the bus.

〈정답과 해설 29P〉

Study 04 원인을 나타내는 부사절
because – ~ 때문에

> **Because** 주어+동사 ~, 주어+동사 ~.
> (= 주어+동사~ **because** 주어+동사 ~)
> → 주어+동사~, **so** 주어+동사 ~

- **Because** the bike was expensive, I didn't buy it.
  = I didn't buy the bike **because** it was expensive.
  → The bike was expensive, **so** I didn't buy it.

  그 자전거가 비쌌기 때문에 나는 사지 않았다.

- **Because** I had a cold, I went to see a doctor.
  = I went to see a doctor **because** I had a cold.
  → I had a cold, **so** I went to see a doctor.

  내가 감기에 걸렸기 때문에 나는 진찰받기 위해 갔다.

- **Because** they won the game, they were very happy.
  = They were very happy **because** they won the game.
  → They won the game, **so** they were very happy.

  그들이 게임을 이겼기 때문에 그들은 매우 행복했다.

- **Because** Kevin was sick, he didn't come to the meeting.
  = Kevin didn't come to the meeting **because** he was sick.
  → Kevin was sick, **so** he didn't come to the meeting.

  Kevin이 아팠기 때문에 그는 회의에 오지 않았다.

- The diners were happy **because** they could eat their pheasant.

  식사하는 사람들은 그들의 꿩고기를 먹을 수 있어서 행복했다.

- The heated air rises **because** warm air is lighter than cool air.

  따뜻한 공기는 시원한 공기보다 가볍기 때문에 가열된 공기는 상승하다.

확인문제 17

다음 because로 연결된 문장에서 부사절에 밑줄 긋고 해석하시오.

(01). He was absent today because he was ill.

  → _____

(02). Because the book is so interesting, I read it.

  → _____

(03). People likes Peter because he is very friendly.

  → _____

(04). Anne couldn't take a field trip because she was ill.

  → _____

(05). Because I studied hard, I got an A$^+$ on the exam.

  → _____

(06). My son raises many birds because he loves animals.

  → _____

(07). We had to come back home because it was too cold.

  → _____

(08). Because it is a holiday, you don't have to go to school.

  → _____

(09). We didn't enjoy the day because the weather was so bad.

  → _____

(10). I can't go to the cinema because I have to take care of the baby.

  → _____

〈정답과 해설 29~30P〉

Study 05 상황상관없음에 해당하는 부사절
though/ although

---

though, although: 상황상관없음(양보): ∼ 할지라도

> **Though/Although 주어+동사 ∼, 주어+동사 ∼**
>
> **→ 주어+동사 ∼, but 주어+동사 ∼**

- Though Annie was poor, she was happy.
  → Annie was poor, but she was happy.　　　Annie는 가난 했지만 그녀는 행복했다.

- Although I have no money, I want to buy the car.
  → I have no money, but I want to buy the car.

　　　　　나는 돈을 가지고 있지 않지만 나는 그 차를 사는 것을 원한다.

🔍 확인문제 18

다음 문장을 though를 사용하여 다시 쓰시오.

(01). I am young, but I know everything.

→ _____

(02). He is wealthy, but he is not happy.

→ _____

(03). Judy made some mistakes, but she won the first prize.

→ _____

(04). Gilbert got up late, but he wasn't late for school.

→ _____

(05). Anne was sick, but she wasn't absent from school.

→ _____

(06). Tom studied hard, but he got poor grades.

    → _____

(07). Beethoven lost his hearing, but he composed many works.

    → _____

(08). They were injured, but they did their best to the end.

    → _____

(09). The weather is bad, but we enjoyed the day at the park.

    → _____

(10). The playground was very small, but it looked large to the little boy.

    → _____

〈정답과 해설 30P〉

확인문제 19

다음 문장을 but을 사용하여 다시 쓰시오. 그리고 해석하시오.

(01). Though he is short, he plays basketball well.

    → _____

    해석) _____

(02). Though he was ill, he never gave up his dream.

    → _____

    해석) _____

(03). Although the wind blew hard, the old man went out to the sea to fish.

    → _____

    해석) _____

(04). Though Beethoven lost his hearing, he composed many works.

    → _____

    해석) _____

〈정답과 해설 30P〉

Study 06 결과에 해당하는 부사절

'so ～ that 주어 + 동사 ～ ': – 너무 ～해서 ～하다.

- Lydia is **so** strong **that** she can lift the heavy box.

  Lydia는 너무나 강해서 그녀는 무거운 박스를 들 수 있다.

- Franklin was **so** tired **that** he couldn't do the homework.

  Franklin은 너무나 피곤해서 그는 숙제를 할 수 없었다.

- I was **so** tired **that** I couldn't do the homework.

  나는 너무 피곤해서 숙제를 할 수 없었다.

확인문제 20

다음 문장을 해석하시오.

(01). The table was so heavy that I couldn't move it.

→ _____

(02). The questions are so difficult that I can't answer them.

→ _____

(03). This book was so interesting that I read it three times.

→ _____

(04). It was so hot that I took a cold shower.

→ _____

(05). I was so busy that I couldn't answer the phone.

→ _____

(06). The task was so easy that she could do it quickly.

→ _____

(07). The weather is so hot that people can't go out.

→ _____

(08). This water is so cold that I can feel cool in no time.

→ _____

(09). This computer is so latest that students can use it easily.

→ _____

(10). This cake was so hard that I couldn't eat it.

→ _____

〈정답과 해설 30P〉

'~ so ~ that 주어 can~ '은 '~ 형용사/부사 enough to 동사원형 ~'으로 문장을 간단히 할 수 있다.

~ so 형용사/부사 that 주어 can ~

→ 형용사/부사 enough to 동사원형 ~

- He is so strong that he can lift the box.
  → He is strong enough to lift the box.　　　　그는 너무 강해서 그 상자를 들 수 있다.

또 '~ so ~ that 주어 can't ~ '은 '~ too 형용사/부사 to 동사원형 ~'으로 문장을 간단히 할 수 있다.

~ so 형용사/부사 that 주어 can't ~

→ too 형용사/부사 to 동사원형 ~

- She was so nervous that she couldn't sleep well.
  → She was too nervous to sleep well.　　　　그녀는 너무나 초조해서 잘 잘 수가 없었다.

 확인문제 21

다음 두 문장의 뜻이 같도록 빈칸에 알맞은 말을 쓰시오.

(01). Jack is so strong that he can lift the box.
　　　→ Jack is strong _____ lift the box.

(02). Annie was so young that he couldn't read the book.
　　　→ Annie was _____ young _____ read the book.

(03). Alice was so nervous that she couldn't sleep well.
　　　→ Alice was _____ nervous _____ sleep well.

(04). Andrew is so thin that he can get through the door.
　　　→ Andrew is thin _____ get through the door.

《정답과 해설 30P》

Chapter 09 부사절

Study 07 목적을 나타내는 부사절
so that 주어 + can/ will/ may 동사원형

'so(in order) that 주어 can/will/may 동사원형 ~'은 'so as(in order) to 동사원형'으로 간단히 할 수 있다.

> **so(=in order) that + 주어 + can/ will/ may(과거일 때는 could/ would/ might) 동사원형 ~: -~ 하기 위하여 ~하다**
>   **→ (so as/ in order) to 동사원형**

- He works hard so that he may succeed in life.   그는 인생에서 성공하기 위하여 열심히 일한다.
  → He works hard so as to succeed in life.
- They sat by the window so that they could see outside better.

   그들은 바깥을 좀 더 잘 볼 수 있도록 창가에 앉았다.

  → They sat by the window so as to see outside better.

확인문제 22

다음 문장을 'so that'에 유의하여 해석하시오.
(01). They went to China so that they might learn Chinese.

   → _____

(02). I hurried so that I could take a train on time.

   → _____

(03). She held the door open so that I could walk through.

   → _____

(04). I provide bicycles for them so that they can attend school.

   → _____

(05). The professor collect a lot of data so that he may write a book.

   → _____

(06). Jane ran out so that she could catch a taxi.

　　→ _____

(07).　I went to Canada so that I could learn English.

　　→ _____

(08). We climbed higher so that we could get a better view.

　　→ _____

(09). I studied hard so that I could get a good grade.

　　→ _____

(10). Dan and I are taking tennis lessons so that we can lose some weight.

　　→ _____

〈정답과 해설 30~31P〉

🔍 확인문제 23

다음 각 두 문장을 ' ～ so that ～' 형식으로 한 문장으로 연결하시오. 그리고 해석하시오.

(01). I studied hard. + I could pass the exam.

　　→ _____

　　해석) _____

(02). We went early. + We could get good seats.

　　→ _____

　　해석) _____

(03). He worked hard. + His family could live in comfort.

　　→ _____

　　해석) _____

(04). He went to bed early. + He could get up early tomorrow.

　　→ _____

　　해석) _____

(05). The patients go out the hospital. + They may take a walk everyday.

　　→ _____

　　해석) _____

〈정답과 해설 30~31P〉

Study 08 두 가지 이상의 뜻으로 쓰이는 부사절
since, as

1. since: ~ 때문에 OR ~한 이후로

① ~ 때문에(because)

- Since Willy is sick, he can't go to school.   Willy가 아프기 때문에 그는 학교에 갈 수 없다.

② ~ 한 이후로

- The players have exercised in the field since they got up in the morning early.

그 선수들은 아침에 일찍 일어난 이후로 운동장에서 운동하고 있다.

확인문제 24

다음 문장을 since에 유념하여 해석하시오.

(01). Since he was sick, he didn't go to the concert.

→ _____

(02). Queen Victoria has been in mourning since her husband died in 1861.

→ _____

(03). Willy is worried about grandfather's health, since Grandfather isn't eating very much these days.

→ _____

〈정답과 해설 31P〉

2. as: ～할 때, ～ 때문에, ～하면서, ～처럼, ～만큼, ～함에 따라서

① ～ 할 때(=when)

- The man said to the woman **as** they walked away.　　그들이 떠날 때, 그 남자는 그 여자에게 말했다.
- Billy was quiet **as** they walked back to the monkey house.

　　그들이 원숭이 집으로 되돌아 걸어 올 때, Billy는 조용했다.

- **As** they were crossing the street, they heard someone call to them.

　　그들이 거리를 가로 지르고 있을 때, 그들은 누군가가 그들을 부르는 것을 들었다.

- The man said "amazing" **as** Cam opened her eyes.

　　Cam이 그녀의 눈을 떴을 때, 그 남자는 "amazing" 이라고 말했다.

- **As** little Will reached the door, Clifford Snyder again aimed his gun at Searchlight.

　　어린 Will이 문에 도착했을 때, Clifford Snyder는 다시 Searchlight를 목표로 그의 총을 겨눴다.

② ～ 때문에(=because)

- **As** it was too late, I turned back.　　너무 늦었기 때문에 나는 돌아왔다.

③ ～ 하면서

- Clifford Snyder began his work **as** he lit up a long, thin cigar.

　　Clifford Synder 길고 가는 시가에 불을 붙이면서 그의 일을 시작했다.

- **As** John Graham fell ill, Annie offered to take the place.

　　John Graham이 아프게 되면서 Annie는 자리를 대신할 것을 제안했다.

④ ～ 만큼

- No monkey is as smart **as** my friend Eric is.　　어떤 원숭이도 내 친구 Eric만큼 영리하지 않다.

⑤ ～ 함에 따라서

- **As** it gets colder, people look for a hot drink more.

　　날씨가 추워짐에 따라서 사람들은 따뜻한 음료를 더 많이 찾는다.

전치사 as: ～로서

- Some people keep geese **as** pets.

　　얼마간의 사람들은 거위를 애완동물로서 기른다.

- Judy gave the doll to me **as** a gift.

　　Judy는 나에게 인형을 선물로 주었다.

- The Koreans regard Kimchi **as** a national food.

　　한국인들은 김치를 국민음식으로 간주한다.

확인문제 25

아래 문장에서 as에 유념하여 해석하시오.

(01). <u>As</u> we have more, we want more.

→ _____

(02). His sister is <u>as</u> beautiful <u>as</u> she has been expected to be.

→ _____

(03). The players think of him <u>as</u> their hero.

→ _____

(04). <u>As</u> the crowd watched, he and Annie began shooting.

→ _____

(05). <u>As</u> he turned, he took the ball out of his pocket.

→ _____

(06). <u>As</u> we have no money to buy books, we lend ones in the library.

→ _____

(07). Little Willy waved a good-bye hand <u>as</u> Searchlight started off down Main Street.

→ _____

(08). <u>As</u> little Willy hitched Searchlight to the sled, something down at the end of street caught his eye.

→ _____

(09). <u>As</u> Cam put the camera in her bag, a young man ran past.

→ _____

(10). <u>As</u> Eric walked past a large wooden area, he heard the sounds of twigs breaking.

→ _____

〈정답과 해설 31P〉

Study 09 기타 부사절을 이끄는 접속사들
like, wherever, however, whoever, whatever

1. like : ~처럼, ~같이

- Billy made a funny face, like he was eating poison.
  Billy는 독극물을 먹고 있는 것처럼 웃기는 표정을 했다.

CF 강조시 as나 like앞에 just를 붙여 just as, just like 꼭 ~처럼
- Eric and Billy ran toward the monkey house door just as Cam was coming in.
  막 Cam이 들어오고 있을 때, Eric and Billy가 원숭이 집 문을 향하여 달렸다.
- Just as we were about to escape over the fence, the strange man in white came running after us.
  막 우리가 울타리 위로 피하려 했을 때, 흰옷을 입은 이상한 남자가 우리를 쫓으며 달려왔다.
- The fur kept in the heat, just like the paper under our jackets kept in our body heat.
  꼭 우리 재킷아래 종이가 우리 몸 열을 유지해주었던 것처럼, 모피가 열을 유지해 주었다.

2. wherever : 어디라도

- Wherever you may go, your family will be with you.
  네가 어디를 가든, 너의 가족이 함께 할 것이다.

3. whenever : 언제라도

- I will help you whenever you want some help.
  네가 도움을 원할 때면 언제든지 내가 도와줄게.

4. however : 아무리 ~라도

- However tired you may be, you must finish the work.
  아무리 피곤하더라도 너는 그 일을 끝내야 한다.

5. whoever : 누구라 하더라도

- **Whoever** may win in the election, he must face many challenges.

    누가 선거에서 이긴다고 하더라도 그는 많은 도전에 직면해야만 한다.

6. whatever : 무엇이라 하더라도

- **Whatever** you may do, you must do your best.

    네가 무엇을 한다하더라도 너는 최선을 다해야 한다.

🔍 확인문제 26

다음 문장에서 적절한 접속사를 보기에서 골라 쓰시오. 그리고 해석하시오.

| whoever | whatever | like | wherever | however |

(01). Nobody loves you (　　　　　) I do.

→ _____

(02). When can I draw cartoons well (　　　　　) Mira does?

→ _____

(03). (　　　　　) strong you may be, you can't carry the box.

→ _____

(04). The puppy follows the girl (　　　　　) she goes.

→ _____

(05). (　　　　　) may come, that person will be welcomed.

→ _____

(06). (　　　　　) he may do, he will succeed in it.

→ _____

〈정답과 해설 31P〉

Grammar in Reading

〈정답과 해설 31~32P〉

1. 아래 글에서 (   ) 안에 알맞은 말을 넣으시오.

Hi, I'm Sandy, and this is my pet turtle, Bada. She's very sick. She doesn't move or eat at all. What happened?

Last weekend, her shell looked very dry. So I put her in the water and blocked the sunlight, but she got worse.

Turtles like to swim in the water, but they can't stay in the water very long.
They'll become weak. They also need a lot of sunshine.

Put Bada in the sun more often, (   ) she'll get better soon!

정답- (   )

2. 아래 글을 읽고 빈칸에 알맞은 접속사를 넣으시오.

Weather words are used in many ways. ⓐ (   ) a person makes everyone happy, he or she is called a ray of sunshine. ⓑ (   ) someone runs fast, he or she runs like the wind. ⓒ (   ) people save money for a bad time, they save for a rainy day.

* a ray of sunshine: 한 줄기 햇살

	ⓐ	ⓑ	ⓒ		ⓐ	ⓑ	ⓒ
①	If	If	When	②	As	As	Though
③	Since	As	As	④	Though	Though	As

Grammar in Reading

〈정답과 해설 32P〉

3. 아래 글을 읽고 빈칸에 알맞은 접속사를 넣으시오.

Peter wanted to go out, ⓐ (   ) he could not find his hat. "Will you help me, Mom? I can't find my hat," said Peter. ⓑ (   ) his mother saw him, she began to laugh. "You can't see your hat ⓒ (   ) it is on your head!"

	ⓐ	ⓑ	ⓒ		ⓐ	ⓑ	ⓒ
①	and	As	As	②	If	As	Because
③	but	When	because	④	Though	When	Though

4. 아래 글을 읽고 빈칸에 알맞은 접속사를 넣으시오.

Helen Keller was born in 1880. She became blind and deaf ⓐ (   ) she was a baby. The world was very dark ⓑ (   ) quiet for her. ⓒ (   ) Helen was seven, she met a great teacher, Annie Sullivan. She taught her how to read and write. Two years later, she could read and write well.

01. ⓐ-   02. ⓑ-   03. ⓒ-

5. 아래 글을 읽고 빈칸에 알맞은 접속사를 넣으시오.

Good morning, everyone. Today, we're going to have an "Apple Day" event during lunch time. It'll take place in the school library. ⓐ (   ) you come, you can see a special desk with apple-shaped cards, coloring pencils, and a book list. There, you can write a sorry card to a friend. Then, choose a book from the book list ⓑ (   ) you want to share with your friend. We'll deliver the book with the card to your friend tomorrow. Don't miss this great chance to build your friendship.

01. ⓐ-   02. ⓑ-

Grammar in Reading

〈정답과 해설 32P〉

6. 아래 글을 읽고 빈칸에 알맞은 접속사를 넣으시오.

Hello, students! This is your principal, Ms. Baker. ⓐ (   ) you know, a typhoon is coming this weekend. There will be strong winds and heavy rain. So, let me tell you what to do to protect your classroom. First, close all the windows ⓑ (   ) you go home. It'll protect your computers and TVs from the rain. Second, don't forget to close the curtains. ⓒ (   ) the window breaks, the curtain will prevent the glass pieces from scattering all over your chairs and desks. Now you see what to do. Have a nice weekend!

01. ⓐ-   02. ⓑ-   03. ⓒ-

7. 아래 글을 읽고 빈칸에 알맞은 접속사를 넣으시오.

Trees are very important to us. Their leaves give fresh air. ⓐ (   ) the leaves fall to the ground, they help other plants to grow. ⓑ (   ) there are no more trees, the land will become a desert. Then our lives will be in danger.

	ⓐ	ⓑ			ⓐ	ⓑ
①	When	Though		②	When	When
③	Though	Though		④	That	When

〈정답과 해설 32~33P〉

1. 다음 우리말에 맞게 괄호 안의 단어를 바르게 배열하시오.

01. 그가 노력했지만 그는 바위를 들 수 없었다.
   (the rock, though, could, not, lift, he, tried, he)
   → _____

02. 그들이 너무 가난했지만 그들은 행복했다.
   (they, were, poor, they, were, so, though, happy)
   → _____

03. 너무나 추웠지만 그는 코트 없이 나갔다.
   (went, out, he, without, it, was, though, so, cold, a coat)
   → _____

04. 비가 내리고 있었음에도, 우리는 운동장에서 축구를 했다.
   (it, played, though, the, we, soccer, on, was, raining, playground).
   → _____

05. 비록 Betty가 나를 친절하게 대하진 않지만, 나는 그녀를 매우 많이 좋아한다.
   (Betty, like, much, treat, very, I, doesn't, me, though, kindly, her).
   → _____

06. 비록 그 집은 붕괴되었지만, 아무도 다치지 않았어요.
   (house, the, hurt, was, even, though, one, was, no, destroyed).
   → _____

07. 그녀의 책들은 이해하기 쉽지 않지만, 나는 그 책들을 읽는 것을 즐긴다.
   (books, reading, them, understand, her, to, easy, are, not, although, enjoy, I).
   → _____

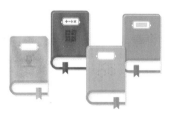

〈정답과 해설 32~33P〉

2. 다음 <보기>와 같이 'so ~ that…' 구문을 이용하여 두 문장을 한 문장으로 연결하시오.

> It was very cold. I couldn't go camping.
> → It was so cold that I couldn't go camping.

01. The table was very heavy. I couldn't move it.
→ _____

02. The questions are very difficult. I can't answer them.
→ _____

03. This book is very interesting. I read it three times.
→ _____

04. It was very hot. I took a cold shower.
→ _____

05. I was very busy. I couldn't answer the phone.
→ _____

06. It was very easy. She could do it quickly.
→ _____

07. The weather is very hot. People can't go out.
→ _____

08. This water is very cold. I can feel cool in no time.
→ _____

09. This computer is very new. Students can use it easily.
→ _____

10. This cake was very hard. I couldn't eat it.
→ _____

〈정답과 해설 33P〉

3. 다음 두 문장의 뜻이 같게 할 때 빈 칸에 알맞은 말은?

01. Get up early, and you will feel better.
 → If _____

02. Be honest, and you will have good luck.
 → If _____

03. Wait here, and you will meet the king.
 → If _____

04. Go now, and you will take the bus.
 → If _____

05. Take on the bus, or you will be late for school.
 → If _____
 → Unless _____

06. Go right now, or you can't see her.
 → If _____
 → Unless _____

07. Work hard, or you won't succeed.
 → If _____
 → Unless _____

08. Depart now, or you'll miss the train.
 → If _____
 → Unless _____

09. Hurry up, or you will miss the bus.
 → If _____
 → Unless _____

10. Exercise every day, or you will get weight.
 → If _____
 → Unless _____

4. 다음 문장을 '명령문, and/or ~'와 'If 주어 ~'형식으로 영작하시오. 필요한 경우 'Unless 주어 ~'
형식으로도 영작하시오.

01. 열심히 공부해라, 그러면 시험에 합격할 것이다.(pass the entrance exam)
   → _____
   → _____

02. 지도를 따라 가거라, 그러면 곰을 만나게 될 거야.(follow the map, meet a bear)
   → _____
   → _____

03. 코너에서 왼쪽으로 돌아라, 그러면 우체국을 볼 것이다.(turn left at the corner)
   → _____
   → _____

04. 이 길을 따라 가거라, 그러면 너는 주차장에 도착 할 것이다. (follow this lane, get to the parking lot.)
   → _____
   → _____

05. 빨리 달려라, 그러면 너는 서울행 마지막 열차를 탈 수 있을 것이다. (catch the last train for Seoul)
   → _____
   → _____

06. 찾아라, 그러면 답을 찾을 것이다. (seek, find the answer)
   → _____
   → _____

07. 물어라, 그러면 너는 마음의 세계에 키를 받을 것이다. (ask, be given, the key, to this world of mind)
   → _____
   → _____

08. 일찍 일어나라. 그렇지 않으면 늦을 것이다.(get up, be late)
   → _____
   → _____
   → _____

〈정답과 해설 34P〉

09. 열심히 공부해라. 그렇지 않으면 인생에 성공하지 못할 것이다.(succeed in life)

　→ _____

　→ _____

　→ _____

10. 여기에서 기다려라. 그렇지 않으면 그녀를 만나지 못할 것이다.(wait here, see)

　→ _____

　→ _____

　→ _____

5. 다음 (　　　)안에 before, after, until, since 중 가장 알맞은 것 하나를 골라 쓰시오.

01. Wait in the classroom (　　　　　) your teacher comes.

02. It gets dark, (　　　　　) the sun set.

03. (　　　　　) I graduate, I'll work at computer company.

04. Let's meet at the gate (　　　　　) school is over.

05. The old lady went on writing (　　　　　) she died.

06. You should go now, (　　　　　) you miss the train.

07. (　　　　　) the camera hit the ground, I caught it.

08. (　　　　　) his father died, Willy has lived in the grass field.

09. (　　　　　) she had a hearty lunch, Annie spent the afternoon rehearsing.

10. Annie practiced her reading and writing (　　　　　) she could do both without a struggle.

〈정답과 해설 34P〉

6. 다음 괄호 안에 주어진 접속사 중 알맞은 것을 고르시오.

01. [If/Whether] you open the door, a loud bell sounds.

02. [If/Unless] you hurry, maybe we can't catch the last train.

03. Doc Smith will be in good hands [until/unless] the end comes.

04. You can't succeed in life, [unless/if] you work hard.

05. Susan had dinner [after/until] she finished her homework.

06. The food should be ready [before/though] the customers arrive.

07. [Unless/If] you can pay for the bill, you must go out of this room.

08. Our friends stay on the bus [while/unless] we have our lunch.

09. [When/That] she says that, she remembers everything.

10. Driving a wagon at night is hard [if/whether] there's no full moon.

11. Jocob Moses died of pneumonia [when/what] Annie was five years old.

12. Lester watched the departing sled for a long time [before/if] he yelled, "Good luck, son!"

7. 다음 우리말과 일치하도록 빈칸에 알맞은 말을 쓰시오.

01. 나는 저녁을 먹은 후에 TV를 시청하였다.
= _____ he had dinner, he watched TV.

02. 네가 휴식을 하는 것을 원한다면 우리는 지금 휴식할 수 있다.
= _____ you want to rest, we can rest now.

03. 나는 초등학교를 졸업한 후에 이곳으로 이사 왔다.
= _____ I graduated from elementary school, I moved here.

《정답과 해설 34P》

04. 나는 등교하기 전에 아침 먹을 시간이 없다.
  = I don't have time to eat breakfast _____ I go to school.

05. Kimberly는 청바지를 많이 좋아하기 때문에 스커트를 거의 입지 않는다.
  = Kimberly seldom wears a skirt _____ she likes jeans more.

06. 우리가 보고 있는 동안에 그는 야구공을 다시 바꿨다.
  = _____ we are watching, he switched the baseballs again.

07. 그 감자가 팔릴 때까지 저장 될 것이다.
  = The potatoes will be stored _____ they can be sold.

08. David가 거리에 있을 때 소중한 야구공이 도난당했다.
  = _____ David was in the street, a valuable baseball was stolen.

09. 녹색으로 바뀌었지만, 차들이 움직이지 않았다.
  = _____ the light turned to green, the cars still didn't move.

10. 어린 Willy는 그가 말하기 전 오랫동안 조용했다.
  = Little Willy was silent for a long time _____ he spoke.

11. 식당에서 식사를 한 후에 돈이 없는 걸 알았다.
  = _____ I had dinner at the restaurant, I found that I had no money.

12. 나의 엄마는 내가 수학에 흥미가 없으니 약간 걱정한다.
  = My mother is a little worried _____ I'm not very interested in math.

8. 다음 우리말에 맞게 괄호안의 단어를 적절하게 배열하시오.

01. 그의 엄마가 저녁을 요리하는 동안 그는 밖에서 놀았다.
  (he, while, cooking, played, mother, outside, his, was, dinner)
  → _____

02. 나는 영화를 보는 동안 팝콘 먹는 것을 좋아한다.
  (I, while, like, watch, popcorn, I, eating, movies)
  → _____

〈정답과 해설 34P〉

03. 내가 자고 있는 동안 강아지가 내 책을 찢었다.

(I, while, my, sleeping, book, puppy, was, tore, my)

→ _____

04. 그녀가 도착 했을 때, 그는 잠자고 있는 중이었다.

(sleeping, was, when, she, he, arrived)

→ _____

05. 날씨가 추워서 그는 창문을 닫았다.

(because, he, the window, cold, it, closed, was)

→ _____

06. 나는 Park 선생님의 수업이 재미있어서 그분의 수업을 좋아한다.

(fun, I, his class, like, Mr. Park's class, is, because)

→ _____

07. 셔츠가 더러워져서 그녀는 그것을 세탁했다.

(the shirt, she, washed, dirty, got, because, it)

→ _____

08. 그가 한국에 머무는 동안 그는 서울에서 그의 시간을 대부분 보냈다.

(his time, in Seoul, while, spent, he, stayed, he, most, of, in Korea)

→ _____

09. 네가 어떤 것을 먹기 전에 너의 손을 씻어라.

(you, something, before, eat, your, hands, wash)

→ _____

10. 나의 아빠는 아침에 일어나자마자 보통 컴퓨터를 켠다.

(my dad, his computer, gets up, usually, turns on, in the morning, as soon as, he)

→ _____

〈정답과 해설 35P〉

9. 다음 문장들을 아래 보기문장처럼 '~so ~ that ~'형식으로 문장을 연결하시오. 그리고 해석하시오.

> The prince found the show very exciting. He stood for most of it.
> → The prince found the show so exciting that he stood for most of it.

01. Lydia is very strong. She can lift the heavy box.
    → _____
    → _____

02. Franklin was very tired. He couldn't do the homework.
    → _____
    → _____

03. The man is very strong. He can lift the heavy box.
    → _____
    → _____

04. I was very tired. I couldn't write a letter.
    → _____
    → _____

05. The soil is becoming very salty. The farmers cannot grow any crops.
    → _____
    → _____

06. The old sled was very light. Little Willy could pick it up with one hand.
    → _____
    → _____

07. The storm was very fierce. The ship lost a propeller and drifted 250 miles off course.
    → _____
    → _____

08. There are very many figures, columns and numbers. He couldn't make any sense out of what he was looking at.
    → _____
    → _____

memo.

중학내신 만점대비
영문법 쏙쏙·영어 쑥쑥

저자 손 창연 선생님 강의 수강 후기들!!

–홈페이지에 실명으로 올린 내용들이나 이름 가운데를 ♥처리 합니다.–

이♥명
다른 영어학원과 차별화된 수업 방식으로 영어를 쉽게 배울 수 있어서 정말 좋다. 문법을 이용한 리딩 수업은 고1 내신대비에도 도움이 될 것 같다.

홍♥우
여태까지 다른 영어학원을 다니면서 항상 문법 쪽에서 약했는데, 이 학원에서 다닌 후로 영어 문법이 훨씬 쉽게 느껴졌다.

이♥빈
나는 홍콩에서 1년 6개월 국제학교 다녔다. 중학교 1학년이다. 2학년 올라간다. 토요일 1회씩 3개월 다녔다. 영어 꽤 한다고 생각했으나 한국어로 문법 개념을 잘 몰라 이 학원에 와서 배우게 되었다.

선생님께서 문법 개념을 쉽고 간단한 용어로 설명해주셔서 내가 이해를 쉽게 할 수 있었다. 또한, 이 수업을 통해 시험 점수가 꽤 올라서 좋았다.

장♥혁
쉽고 재밌게 잘 가르치신다.

김♥영
3개월 수업 후 만점
중 3인데 지난 7월 방학부터 손창연 선생님 수업 3개월 듣고 이번 중간고사 만점 맞았어요. 맨날 80점 초반대 였는데...
손창연 논리문법 강추

오♥현
자세한 영어 문법/ 나는 역삼중학교에 다니는 중학교 3학년 오*현 학생 입니다.평소 시험에 문법 문제를 많이 틀려 이 학원에 다니게 되어있는 데 여기서 만든 문제집은 좁은 단원도 세밀하게 나태내어서 좀더 정확히 이해할수 있고 문제가 광범위해서 평소 다른 학원 에서 풀수 없었던 문법 문제를 많이 풀었다.

신♥규
한국에 와서 영어 수업 큰 도움 되었어요. 한국에 와서 선생님 문법수업듣고 문법에서 정말 도움이 되었던 것 같다. 에세이 쓰는데 큰 도움이 되었다. 부사절을 정리하는 감목결이조, 원조시동상, 장모비비대가 생각난다.

장♥연
쉽고 재미있게, 잘 외울 수 있게 도와주시면서 가르치신다. 수업이 즐겁다.

오♥현
설명을 암기하기 쉽게 해주셔서 나중에 기억할 수 있게 하는게 암기력 떨어지는 저에게 제일 장점인 것 같아요.보통 다 까먹는데 계속 반복하니까 희미하게라도 다시 기억할 수있으니까 더 좋고요.
그런데, 나 독해를 하는 것도 좋지만 저에게는 문법을 확실히 잡으려고 이 원에 온 것이라 문법을 좀 더 더 메인으로 잡고 할 수 있으면 좋겠습니다.

수업은 잘 듣고 있습니다^^

이♥성
너무 읽는 형식의 수업이 지루한감이 있지만 창의적인 문장과 실용적인 수업이 더욱 쉽게 공부를 할 수 있게 만든다.

우♥호
원래 문법이라는 것 자체가 잘못하면 굉장히 지루하고 어려워서 히기 싫온 미음이 많이 듭 수 있지만 손창연 선생님의 수업은 오히려 문법에 흥미를 갖게 해줍니다!!

열정적인 선생님과 그 선생님의 특별하고 재미있는 수업을 받으면 정말 영어문법을 잘 할 수 있게 될 것입니다.

seeenglish.com

중학내신만점대비
영문법 쏙쏙·영어 쑥쑥

저자 손 창연 선생님 강의 수강 후기들!!

–홈페이지에 실명으로 올린 내용들이나 이름 가운데를 ♥처리 합니다.–

임♥현
원래문법이 지루한데 더 재미있게 배울 수 있어서 참 좋았어요
신기한 암기법으로 더 머리에 쏙쏙 들어 오니깐 좋은 것 같다.
열정적으로 가르치니깐 좋다.

홍♥우
여태까지 다른 영어학원을 다니면서 항상 문법 쪽에서 약했는데, 이 학원에서 다닌 후로 영어 문법이 훨씬 쉽게 느껴졌다.

박♥철
꼼꼼히 많은 영어 문법을 정리하고 있어요.
저는 현재 태국에서 4년쯤 거주하고 있는 중학요 2학년 학생입니다. 손창연 선생님은 인터넷 서핑과 책들을 통해 알았고 현재 1달 째 다니고 있습니다. 이 학원 좋은 점은 체계적이고 다른 학원과 선생님들에 비해서 비교적 쉬운 가르침 입니다. 대체로 빠른 속도로 영어 맥을 잡아줍니다. 그러나 모든 영어 학원이 그렇지만 다른 학원에서 배우셨다면 이미 배운 내용을 또다시 반복할 수 있기 때문에 선생님한테 살짝 간략하게 설명해달라고 하는 것을 추천합니다.

김♥희
독특한 영어문법 강의...
대치동 아니 전국에서도 찾아볼 수 없는 교수법...정말 좋습니다...

박♥열
중학 교 2학년 입니다.
이 문법학원을 오게된 것은 대원외고를 다니고 미국의 아이비리그에 들어간 친구누나가 이학원을 다녀서 효과를 보았다는 말을 듣고 오게 되었습니다.
처음에는 문법을 배워도 빨리 까먹기 일수였습니다. 그런데 이 문법 책을 보고 공부하고 나니 더 암기도 쉽고, 선생님도 재미있게 가르쳐주어서 문법문제를 풀때 선생님이 알려주셨던 암기노래가 생각나서 더 쉽게 풀 수 있었습니다. 그리고 수업시작하기 전에 전시간에 배웠던 수업을 다시 브리핑하는 시간을 가져서 다시한번 더 복습하고 갈수있게 되었습니다.
그리고 선생님이 쓰신 OEG시리즈 네 권의 많은 문법문제를 풀면서 구문을 배워서 영어의 이치를 알게 되었습니다.

이♥민
영어문법 , 특히 문장의 형식에 대해 확실하게 이해할 수 있는 좋은 수업이었구요, 특별한 손창연 선생님만의 암기법을 이용하니 훨씬 문장의 5형식에 따를 각각의 동사들을 외우기 쉬웠습니다. 간간히 영어문법과 관련된 사회적 이슈나 시사적 사건들을 통해 사회와 가까운 영어문법을 알려주서서 이해가 더 잘 된것 같습니다.

오♥준
특례생인데요...안녕하세요 러시아에서 살다온 고2 특례생입니다. 예전에는 영어 문법이 부족하고 실수도 많이 했는데 손창연 선생님의 강의 덕분에 점차 자신감이 생기는 듯 합니다. 요번 모의고사도 만점받았구요.

윤♥경
쏙쏙 이해되었어요!
어렵다고 생각했던 영어문법이 재밌고, 쉬워졌어요^^ 쌤이 알려주시는 방식대로 외우니 더 쉽고 간단하게 외워지더라구요!전에 헷갈렸던 부분들도 확실하게 알게되고, 친근하게 노래처럼 알려주시니 더 이해도 쏙쏙 되구요 ㅎㅎ
정말 추천입니다~

seeenglish.com